P9-BZD-854

THE
ETHICS
OF
WAR AND PEACE

THE
ETHICS
OF
WAR AND PEACE

Douglas P. Lackey

Baruch College and the Graduate Center
City University of New York

Prentice Hall, Upper Saddle River, New Jersey 07458

LIBRARY OF CONGRESS
Library of Congress Cataloging-in-Publication Data

Lackey, Douglas P.
   The ethics of war and peace / by Douglas P. Lackey.
      p.   cm.
   Bibliography: p.
   Includes index.
   ISBN 0-13-290925-1. (pbk.)   ISBN 0-13-290933-2
   1. War--Moral and ethical aspects.   2. Peace--Moral and ethical
aspects.   I. Title.
U22.L32 1989
172'.42--dc19   88-4818
                                                         CIP

Cover design: Lundgren Graphics, Ltd.
Manufacturing buyer: Margaret Rizzi/Peter Havens

© 1989 by Prentice-Hall, Inc.
A Pearson Education Co.
Upper Saddle River, NJ 07458

All rights reserved. No part of this book may be
reproduced, in any form or by any means,
without permission in writing from the publisher.

Printed in the United States of America

ISBN 0-13-290925-1 (PBK)

ISBN 0-13-290933-2

Prentice-Hall International (UK) Limited,London
Prentice-Hall of Australia Pty. Limited, Sydney
Prentice-Hall Canada Inc., Toronto
Prentice-Hall Hispanoamericana, S.A., Mexico
Prentice-Hall of India Private Limited, New Delhi
Prentice-Hall of Japan, Inc., Tokyo
Pearson Education Asia Pte. Ltd., Singapore
Editora Prentice-Hall do Brasil, Ltda., Rio de Janeiro

For My Mother
Anne Dorothy Lackey

CONTENTS

PREFACE

In its presentation of theories, this book seeks to develop and analyze all leading points of view. But in the course of describing many concrete examples of wars and battles from 1914 to the present, I have not shrunk from giving my own opinions about the moral character of what was done. Readers are encouraged to agree or disagree as they see fit. I think it is better for readers to encounter personal opinions backed by deep and considered feelings than an objective pretense that encourages the idea that no question can ever be settled.

Readers will notice that I have concentrated my criticisms on actions of the United States and the allies of the United States, particularly the state of Israel. I say little about actions by opponents of the United States, for example, the Soviet Union's invasions of Hungary, Czechoslovakia, and Afghanistan. There are two reasons for this selectiveness. First, these Soviet invasions were so blatantly immoral that they leave little room for analysis or debate, only condemnation. Second, as an American citizen, I feel morally responsible for actions taken by the United States, not for actions taken by the Soviets. As an American citizen, I also feel indirectly responsible for actions taken by the state of Israel, which every year receives over three billion dollars in American aid.

Nevertheless, readers may be disturbed by a certain lack of patriotic spirit in my discussions of American wars. Patriotic spirit has its place, but like everything else it must be subjected to philosophical criticism. Philosophers must be citizens of the world, and the rules of ethics are without nationality.

In preparing this volume, I am indebted to William Earle, who carefully read the whole book through in manuscript, and to James Rachels for his suport of this project and his encouragement over the years.

1
INTRODUCTION

International Ethics and the Challenge of Realism

A philosophical book devoted to the subject of war and peace might choose to concentrate on metaphysical questions, such as the nature of war, the function of war in human history, or the meaning of war in human life. But in this book we will be interested primarily in ethical questions, not metaphysical ones. Is war ever morally justified? Is there a morally correct way of fighting a war? Is it morally permissible to threaten immoral uses of force in order to secure some morally admirable goal? These and similar ethical questions about war have been debated for centuries, but no consensus about them has emerged. In an age of nuclear weapons, they are more pressing than ever before.

Before we enter into these moral debates, a preliminary problem must be addressed. Some thinkers have maintained that conflict *within* a society can be morally assessed and regulated, but that conflict *between* societies cannot. The reason is that within one society there is a common moral system, but between two societies there is no common moral standard, no mutually accepted procedure for reaching moral conclusions, and no common judiciary for enforcing moral judgments. From considerations like these, some conclude that all is fair in love and war and that, as regards international affairs, moral discussion is just wasted words, at least until the day that world government arrives.

I would not have written this book if I did not consider this view to be utterly mistaken. The doctrine that moral assessment is useless or pernicious in international affairs, usually dubbed "realism" by political scientists, is the opposite of traditional philosophical realism, which asserts the objective existence of abstract properties, including moral properties. The bogus "realism" of political science is, in fact, a subvariety of the subjectivist interpretation of moral judgments—excusable, perhaps, among middle-class college freshmen, but rejected by the majority of contemporary students of ethics. It is not possible, in this book, to consider all the arguments about the subjectivity of ethics, but it is possible to say a little about why subjectivism regarding moral judgments in international affairs is not as justifiable as political "realists" believe.

First of all, what we are primarily assessing when we consider the ethics of war and peace are the actions and policies of our own political leaders. Ethics is an intensely practical subject, and from the political branch of ethics we seek guidance about what we as a nation ought to do. Only secondarily are we concerned with reaching moral judgments about the actions of political leaders in other nations, and we assess others primarily to assist ourselves in deciding what is right in our own case. Thus the fact that other societies have different standards and may be inclined to reject our conclusions is not a problem for our own ethical deliberations. It follows that the fact that there is no world government and no substantial mechanism of international enforcement, though a major obstacle for international law, is not a problem for international ethics. When we reach moral conclusions, we will be directing them primarily at ourselves, and we can certainly "obey" our own verdicts, even in the absence of world government.

Second, the very fact that we engage in debates about the morality of our policies indicates that we are not simply applying the conventional beliefs of our own society to the solution of these problems. When we judge the actions of our highest political authorities, we are judging our society as a whole, and thereby show our own deep belief in standards that are "outside" our present social system: we show that current social attitudes do not have the last moral word. Many people are subjectivists in the classroom but, confronted with real decisions, they feel the tug of genuine moral standards despite themselves. One senses a commitment to transcendent moral standards on almost every page written by George Kennan, even though publicly and theoretically he endorses a "realistic" moral stance in the assessment of international affairs and conflict.

Third, there is something a little mysterious about a "realism" that maintains that interpersonal conflict can be morally judged but that international conflict cannot. The actions of states are, after all, reducible to the actions of people. The actions of political leaders may require different standards of judgment because of the special obligations that political roles entail, but it does not follow that the human beings who fill those roles are subject to no moral standards at all, as if they suddenly ceased to be human, no longer choosing freely and bearing responsibility for their choices. Because of their roles, parents are permitted certain liberties with their children that are forbidden to strangers. It hardly follows from these liberties (for example, the liberty to choose where the children shall live) that there are no moral standards by which the conduct of parents can be judged. Likewise, political leaders have certain liberties (for example, the liberty to dissimulate during diplomatic discussions) as a result of their roles, but it hardly follows from these liberties that they cannot be judged morally as politicians and as human beings.

Fourth and finally, it is simply incorrect to say that there are no standards between nations for the arbitration of international conflicts. In fact there are common standards of international law and morality, standards developed by many thinkers over many centuries in many different countries. Not every nation subscribes to these standards, and no nation subscribes to all of them, but most subscribe to most of them: even Hitler, for most of World War II, kept to the Geneva Conventions regarding prisoners of war. This body of international doctrine, called the theory of just war, is the primary point of reference for the third and fourth chapters of this book.

This book endorses no single moral code, nor does it judge theories and cases from a single moral viewpoint. Instead, the author seeks to develop *moral considerations* relevant to assessing the theories and judging the cases. The principal moral considerations developed here concern the effect of an issue on the common good, and the relation of an issue to moral rights. No attempt is made to develop a theory of virtuous conduct, or a sample list of virtues for political leaders or for soldiers. Though there is much contemporary discussion of "professionalism" in political and military life, professional codes do not constitute morality and may blunt sensitivity to moral concerns.

"The common good" is the good of everyone affected by a policy, with each person counting as one and nobody as more than one. American newspapers may give more space to a local automobile crash that kills five than a South American mudslide that kills 500, but the moral critic must struggle to overcome this sort of near-sightedness.

"Moral rights" include the basic natural rights to life and liberty, and such rights as derive from contracts and voluntary agreements. (If we make an agreement, those with whom we make it have a right to expect it kept.) Obviously, morality presumes that it is not permissible to violate a right if so doing will secure advantages for someone at the expense of the common good. We will also assume that, in most cases, it is not permissible to violate a right even if so doing will *serve* the common good. But we will not assume the controversial point that it is permissible to take any action necessary in order to secure one's rights. Your right to life, for example, is the right not to be killed, even if killing you will serve the common good. But your right to life is not a right to take whatever you need in order to stay alive, if what you need is something to which others have a right. Finally, we take the uncontroversial view that moral rights can be forfeited by misconduct or waived by free choice.

When all moral considerations relevant to an issue have been canvassed, the moral critic moves on to a considered final judgment. Since different moral considerations often have incomparable weights, the final judgment is made not so much by rules as by an exercise of that practical wisdom that Aristotle called *phronesis.* But even practical wisdom must bow before the rule of logical consistency. In the moral arena, logical consistency means that if a moral judgment about a particular case has been reached on the basis of moral considerations, then the same judgment should be reached regarding all other cases to which the same moral considerations apply. The rule of consistency, or "universalizability," forbids racism, nationalism, and other "isms" from entering into moral assessments, and provides moral judges with a stern test of their purity of heart.

SUGGESTIONS FOR FURTHER READING

For a very sophisticated presentation of the argument that moral judgments of any importance require concepts which derive their meaning from a web of relations within a particular society—and hence are not generalizable to other societies—see Bernard Williams, *Ethics and the Limits of Philosophy* (Cambridge, MA: Harvard University Press, 1985). The skepticism this argument engenders is illustrated in Williams' discussion of the morality of nuclear deterrence, "Morality, Scepticism, and the Nuclear Arms Race," in Nigel Blake and Kay Pole, eds., *Objections to Nuclear Defense* (London: Routledge and Kegan Paul, 1984). For criticism of Williams' position, see Warren Quinn, "Reflection and the Loss of Moral Knowledge," *Philosophy and Public Affairs* (Spring 1987). For more contemporary discussion of the objectivity of moral knowledge, see David Coop and David Zimmerman, eds., *Morality, Reason, and Truth* (Totowa, NJ: Rowman and Allanheld, 1985).

The standard presentation of moral realism in international affairs is Hans Morgenthau, *Politics Among Nations* (New York: Knopf, 1949). See also Henry Kissinger, "Force and Diplomacy in the Nuclear Age," *Foreign Affairs* (April 1956); Colin Gray, *Strategic Studies and Social Policy* (Lexington: University of Kentucky Press, 1982); and Thomas Nagel's quasi-utilitarian realism in "Ruthlessness in Public Life," in Stuart Hampshire, ed., *Public and Private Morality* (Cambridge: Cambridge University Press, 1978).

George Kennan's mixture of theoretical realism and practical moralism is displayed in *The Nuclear Delusion* (New York: Viking, 1982). The sternest Kennan comments in a realistic vein are in private letters quoted in J. E. Hare and Carey Joynt, *Ethics and International Affairs* (New York: St. Martin's Press, 1982); see also Kennan's "Ethics and Foreign Policy," in Theodore Hesburgh and Louis J. Halle, eds., *Foreign Policy and Morality: Framework for a Moral Audit* (New York: Council on Religion and International Relations, 1979). Kennan's latest theoretical statement on the issue, which derives moral egoism in international affairs from the role obligations of diplomats, is "Morality and Foreign Policy," *Foreign Affairs* (Winter 1985/86).

The applicability of moral standards to international affairs is defended in Michael Walzer, *Just and Unjust Wars* (New York: Basic Books, 1977); Charles Beitz, *Political Theory and International Relations* (Princeton, NJ: Princeton University Press, 1979); Henry Shue, *Basic Rights* (Princeton, NJ: Princeton University Press, 1980); Hare and Joynt, *Ethics and International Affairs*; Terry Nardin, *Morality, Law, and the Relations of States* (Princeton, NJ: Princeton University Press, 1983); Gary L. Scott and Craig L. Carr, "Are States Moral Agents?" *Social Theory and Practice* (Spring 1986); and in many of the essays in Charles Beitz, Marshall Cohen, Thomas Scanlon, and A. John Simmons, eds., *International Ethics* (Princeton, NJ: Princeton University Press, 1985).

2
PACIFISM

---

1. VARIETIES OF PACIFISM

Everyone has a vague idea of what a pacifist is, but few realize that there are many kinds of pacifists. (Sometimes the different kinds quarrel with each other!) One task for the student of international ethics is to distinguish the different types of pacifism and to identify which types represent genuine moral theories.

Most of us at some time or other have run into the "live and let live" pacifist, the person who says, "I am absolutely opposed to killing and violence—but I don't seek to impose my own code on anyone else. If other people want to use violence, so be it. They have their values and I have mine." For such a person, pacifism is one life style among others, a life style committed to gentleness and care, and opposed to belligerence and militarism. Doubtless, many people who express such commitments are sincere and are prepared to live by their beliefs. At the same time, it is important to see why "live and let live" pacifism does not constitute a moral point of view.

When someone judges that a certain action, A, is morally wrong, that judgment entails that no one should do A. Thus, there is no way to have moral values without believing that these values apply to other people. If a person says that A is morally wrong but that it doesn't matter if other people do A, then that person either is being inconsistent or doesn't know what the word "moral" means. If a person believes that killing, in certain circumstances, is morally wrong, that belief implies that no one should kill, at least in those circumstances. If a pacifist claims that killing is wrong in *all* circumstances,.but that it is permissible for other people to kill on occasion, then he has not understood the universal character of genuine moral principles. If pacifism is to be a moral theory, it must be prescribed for all or prescribed for none.

Once one recognizes this "universalizing" character of genuine moral beliefs, one will take moral commitments more seriously than those who treat a moral code as a personal life-style. Since moral principles apply to everyone, we must take care that our moral principles are correct, checking that they are not inconsistent with each other, developing and adjusting them so that they are detailed and subtle enough to deal with a variety of circumstances, and making sure that they are defensible against the objections of those who do not accept them. Of course many pacifists do take the business of morality seriously and advance pacifism as a genuine moral position, not as a mere life-style. All such serious pacifists believe that *everyone* ought to be a pacifist, and that those who reject pacifism are deluded or wicked. Moreover, they do not simply endorse pacifism; they offer arguments in its defense.

We will consider four types of pacifist moral theory. First, there are pacifists who maintain that the central idea of pacifism is the immorality of killing. Second, there are pacifists who maintain that the essence of pacifism is the immorality of violence, whether this be violence in personal relations or violence in relations between nation-states. Third, there are pacifists who argue that personal violence is always morally wrong but that political violence is sometimes morally right: for example, that it is sometimes morally permissible for a nation to go to war. Fourth and finally, there are pacifists who believe that personal violence is sometimes morally permissible but that war is always morally wrong.

Albert Schweitzer, who opposed all killing on the grounds that life is sacred, was the first sort of pacifist. Mohandas Gandhi and Leo Tolstoy, who opposed not only killing but every kind of coercion and violence, were pacifists of the second sort: I will call such pacifists "universal pacifists." St. Augustine, who condemned self-defense but endorsed wars against heretics, was a pacifist of the third sort. Let us call him a "private pacifist," since he condemned only violence in the private sphere. Pacifists of the fourth sort, increasingly common in the modern era of nuclear and total war, I will call "antiwar pacifists."

2. THE PROHIBITION AGAINST KILLING

(a) The Biblical Prohibition

One simple and common argument for pacifism is the argument that the Bible, God's revealed word, says to all people "Thou shalt not kill" (Exod. 20:13). Some pacifists interpret this sentence as implying that no one should kill under any circumstances, unless God indicates that this command is suspended, as He did when He commanded Abraham to slay Issac. The justification for this interpretation is the words themselves, "Thou shalt not kill," which are presented in the Bible bluntly and without qualification, not only in Exodus but also in Deuteronomy (5:17).

This argument, however, is subject to a great many criticisms. The original language of Exodus and Deuteronomy is Hebrew, and the consensus of scholarship says that the Hebrew sentence at Exodus 20:13, "Lo Tirzach," is best translated as "Thou shalt do no murder," not as "Thou shalt not kill." If this translation is correct, then Exodus 20:13 does not forbid all killing but only those killings that happen to be murders. Furthermore, there are many places in the Bible where God commands human beings to kill in specified circumstances. God announces 613 commandments in all, and these include "Thou shalt not suffer a witch to live" (Exod. 22:18); "He that blasphemeth the name of the Lord . . . shall surely be put to death, and all the congregation shall stone him" (Lev. 24:16); "He that killeth any man shall surely be put to death" (Lev. 24:17); and so forth. It is difficult to argue that these instructions are like God's specific instructions to Abraham to slay Issac: these are general commandments to be applied by many people, to many people, day in and day out. They are at least as general and as divinely sanctioned as the commandment translated "Thou shalt not kill."

There are other difficulties for pacifists who pin their hopes on prohibitions in the Hebrew Bible. Even if the commandment "Thou shalt not kill," properly interpreted, did prohibit all types of killing, the skeptic can ask whether this, by itself, proves that all killing is immoral. First, how do we know that the statements in the Hebrew Bible really are God's word, and not just the guesses of ancient scribes? Second, even if the commandments in the Bible do express God's views, why are we morally bound to obey divine commands? (To say that we will be punished if we do not obey is to appeal to fear and self-interest, not to moral sentiments.) Third, are the commandments in the Old Testament laws for all people, or just laws for the children of Israel? If they are laws for all people, then all people who do not eat unleavened bread for Passover are either deluded or wicked. If they are laws only for the children of Israel, they are religious laws and not moral laws, since they lack the universality that all moral laws must have.

Finally, the argument assumes the existence of God, and philosophers report that the existence of God is not easy to demonstrate. Even many religious believers are more confident of the truth of basic moral judgments, such as "Small children should not be tortured to death for purposes of amusement," than they are confident of the existence of God. For such people, it would seem odd to try to justify moral principles by appeals to religious principles, since the evidence for those religious principles is weaker than the evidence for the moral principles they are supposed to justify.

(b) The Sacredness of Life

There are, however, people who oppose all killing but do not seek justification in divine revelation. Many of these defend pacifism by appeal to the sacredness of life. Almost everyone is struck with wonder when watching the movements and reactions of a newborn baby, and almost everyone can be provoked to awe by the study of living things, great or small. The complexity of the mechanisms found in living bodies, combined with the efficiency with which they fulfill their functions, is not matched by any of the processes in nonliving matter. People who are particularly awe-struck by the beauty of living things infer from these feelings that life is sacred, that all killing is morally wrong.

Different versions of pacifism have been derived from beliefs about the sacredness of life. The most extreme version forbids the killing of any living thing. This view was allegedly held by Pythagoras, and is presently held by members of the Jain religion in India. (Those who think that such pacifists must soon starve to death should note that a life-sustaining diet can easily be constructed from milk, honey, fallen fruit and vegetables, and other items that are consumable without prior killing.) A less extreme view sanctions the killing of plants but forbids the killing of animals. The most moderate view prohibits only the killing of fellow human beings.

There is deep appeal in an argument that connects the sacredness of life with the wrongfulness of taking life. Even people who are not pacifists are often revolted by the spectacle of killing, and most Americans would be unable to eat meat if they had to watch how the animals whose flesh they consume had been slaughtered, or if they had to do the slaughtering themselves. Most people sense that they do not own the world they inhabit and recognize that they are not free to do with the world as they will, that the things in it, most especially living things, are worthy of respect and care. Seemingly nothing could violate the respect living things deserve more than killing, especially since much of the taking of human and nonhuman life is so obviously unnecessary.

But with the introduction of the word "unnecessary" a paradox arises. Sometimes—less often than we think, but sometimes—the taking of some lives will save other lives. Does the principle that life is sacred and ought to be preserved imply that nothing should ever be killed, or does it imply that as much life should be preserved as possible? Obviously pacifists take the former view; nonpacifists, the latter.

The view that killing is wrong because it destroys what is sacred seems to imply that killing is wrong because killing diminishes the amount of good in the world. It seems to follow that if a person can save more lives by killing than by refusing to kill, arguments about the sacredness of life would not show that killing in these circumstances is wrong. (It might be wrong for other reasons.) The more lives saved, the greater the quantity of good in the world.

The difficulty that some killing might, on balance, save lives, is not the only problem for pacifism based on the sacredness of life. If preserving life is the highest value, a value not comparable with other, non-life-preserving goods, it follows that any acts which place life at risk are immoral. But many admirable actions have been undertaken in the face of death, and many less heroic but morally impeccable actions—driving on a road at moderate speed, authorizing a commercial flight to take off, and so forth—place life at risk. In cases of martyrdom in which people choose death over religious conversion, life is just as much destroyed as it is in a common murder. Yet, on the whole, automobile drivers, air traffic controllers, and religious martyrs are not thought to be wicked. Likewise, people on life-sustaining machinery sometimes request that the machines be turned off, on the grounds that quality of life matters more than quantity of life. We may consider such people mistaken, but we hardly think that they are morally depraved.

In answering this objection, the pacifist may wish to distinguish between *killing other people* and *getting oneself killed*, arguing that only the former is immoral. But although there is a genuine distinction between killing and getting killed, the distinction does not entail that killing other people destroys life but getting oneself killed does not. If life is sacred, life, including one's own life, must be preserved at all cost. In many cases, people consider the price of preserving their own lives simply to be too high.

(c) The Right to Life

Some pacifists may try to avoid the difficulties of the "sacredness of life" view by arguing that the essential immorality of killing is that it violates the *right to life* that every human being possesses. If people have a right to life, then it is never morally permissible to kill some people in order to save others, since according to the usual interpretation of rights, it is never permissible to violate a right in order to secure some good.

A discussion of the logic of rights in general and the right to life in particular is beyond the scope of this book. But a number of students of this subject are prepared to argue that the possession of any right implies the permissibility of defending that right against aggression: if this were not so, what would be the point of asserting the existence of rights? But if the possession of a right to life implies the permissibility of defending that right against aggression—a defense that may require killing the aggressor—then the existence of a right to life cannot by itself imply the impermissibility of killing. On this view, the right to life implies the right to self-defense, including violent self-defense. It does not imply pacifism.

3.   UNIVERSAL PACIFISM

(a)   Christian Pacifism

Universal pacifists are morally opposed to all violence, not just to killing. Many universal pacifists derive their views from the Christian Gospels. In the Sermon on the Mount, Christ taught:

> Ye have heard that it hath been said, An eye for an eye, a tooth for a tooth:
>   But I say unto you, that ye resist not evil: but whosoever shall smite thee on the right cheek, turn to him the other also . . . .
>   Ye have heard it said, thou shalt love thy neighbor, and hate thine enemy. But I say unto you, Love your enemies, bless them that curse you, do good to them that hate you. . . . that ye may be the children of your father which is in heaven: for he maketh the sun to rise on the evil and on the good, and sendeth the rain on the just and the unjust. (Matt. 5:38–45)

In the early centuries of the Christian era, it was widely assumed that to follow Christ and to obey His teaching meant that one should reject violence and refuse service in the Roman army. But by the fifth century, after the Roman Empire had become Christian and after barbarian Goths in 410 sacked Rome itself, Church Fathers debated whether Christ really intended that the Empire and its Church should remain undefended. The Church Fathers noticed passages in the Gospels that seem to contradict pacifism:

> Think not that I am come to send peace on earth: I came not to send peace, but a sword.
>   For I am come to set a man at variance against his father, and the daughter against her mother, and the daughter-in-law against her mother-in-law. (Matt. 10: 34–35)

And there are several instances in the Gospels (for instance, Matt. 8:5–10) in which Jesus encounters soldiers and does not rebuke them for engaging in an occupation that is essentially committed to violence. Rather, he argues, "Render unto Caesar the things which are Caesar's; and unto God the things that are God's" (Matt. 22:21). This would seem to include military service, or at least taxes to pay for the army.

A thorough analysis of whether the Gospels command pacifism is beyond the scope of this book. The passages in the Sermon on the Mount seem to be clearly pacifist; yet many eminent scholars have denied the pacifist message. A more interesting question, for philosophy, if not for biblical scholarship, is this: If Jesus did preach pacifism in the Sermon on the Mount, did He preach it as a *moral* doctrine?

Jesus did not view his teaching as replacing the moral law as he knew it:

> Think not that I am come to destroy the law, or the prophets: I am come not to destroy, but to fulfill. . . .
> Till heaven and earth pass, one jot or tittle shall in no wise pass from the law, till all be fulfilled. (Matt. 5:17–18)

Perhaps, then, the prescriptions of the Sermon on the Mount should be interpreted as rules that one must obey in order to follow Christ, or rules that one must follow in order to obtain salvation. But it does not follow from this alone that everyone has an obligation to follow Christ, and it does not follow from this alone that everyone has an obligation to seek salvation. Even Christians will admit that some people have refused to become Christians and have led morally admirable lives nonetheless; and if salvation is a good, one can nevertheless choose to reject it, just as a citizen can neglect to hand in a winning lottery ticket without breaking the law. If so, the prescriptions of the Sermon on the Mount apply only to Christians seeking a Christian salvation. They are not universally binding rules and do not qualify as moral principles.

(b) The Moral Exemplar Argument

Many people and at least one illustrious philosopher, Immanuel Kant, believe that morally proper action consists in choosing to act in such a way that your conduct could serve as an example for all mankind. (It was Kant's genius to recognize that moral conduct is *essentially* exemplary.) Some universal pacifists appeal to this idea, arguing that if everyone were a pacifist, the world would be a much better place than it is now. This is the argument that Leo Tolstoy (1828–1910) used to support the Gospel prescription not to resist evil:

> [Christ] put the proposition of non-resistance to evil in such a way that, according to his teaching, it was to be the foundation of the joint life of men and was to free humanity from the evil that it inflicted on itself. (*My Religion*, Ch. 4) Instead of having the whole life based on violence and every joy obtained and guarded through violence; instead of seeing each one of us punished or inflicting punishment from childhood to old age, I imagined that we were all impressed in word and deed by the idea that vengeance is a very low, animal feeling; that violence is not only a disgraceful act, but also one that deprives man of true happiness . . . .
> I imagined that instead of those national hatreds which are impressed on us under the form of patriotism, instead of those glorifications of murder, called wars . . . that we were impressed with the idea that the recognition of any countries, special laws, borders, lands, is a sign of grossest ignorance. . . .

> Through the fulfillment of these commandments, the life of men will be what every human heart seeks and desires. All men will be brothers and everybody will always be at peace with others, enjoying all the benefits of the world. (*My Religion*, Ch. 6)

Few would deny that if everyone were a pacifist, the world would be a better place, perhaps even a paradise. Furthermore, since the argument is essentially hypothetical, it cannot be refuted (as many nonpacifists believe) by pointing out that not everyone will become a pacifist. The problem is whether this argument can establish pacifism as a moral imperative.

One difficulty with the argument is that it seems to rely on a premise the truth of which is purely verbal. In what way would the world be a better place if people gave up fighting? The most obvious way is that the world would be better because there would be no war. But the statement "If everyone gave up fighting, there would be no war" is true by definition, since "war" implies "fighting." It is difficult to see how a statement that simply relates the meanings of words could tell us something about our moral obligations.

A deeper problem with Tolstoy's argument is that "resist not evil" is not the only rule that would yield paradise if everyone obeyed it. Suppose that everyone in the world subscribed to the principle "Use violence, but only in self-defense." If everyone used violence only in self-defense, the same consequences would follow as would arise from universal acceptance of the rule "Never use violence." Consequently, pacifism cannot be shown to be superior to nonpacifism by noting the good consequences that would undeniably ensue if everyone were a pacifist.

(c) Gandhian Pacifism

Certainly the most interesting and effective pacifist of the twentieth century was Mohandas Gandhi (1869–1948). Though a devout Hindu, Gandhi developed his doctrine of nonviolence from elementary metaphysical concepts that are by no means special to Hinduism:

> Man as an animal is violent but as spirit is nonviolent. The moment he awakes to the spirit he cannot remain violent. Either he progresses towards *ahimsa* [nonviolence] or rushes to his doom. (*Nonviolence in Peace and War*, I, p. 311)

The requirement not to be violent seems wholly negative; sleeping people achieve it with ease. But for Gandhi the essential moral task is not merely to be nonviolent but to use the force of the soul (*satyagraha*, "truth grasping") in a continual struggle for justice. The methods of applied *satyagraha* developed by Gandhi—the weaponless marches, the sit-downs and sit-ins, strikes and boycotts, fasts and prayers—captured the admiration of the world and have been widely copied, most notably by Martin Luther King, Jr., in his campaigns against racial discrimination. According to Gandhi, each person, by engaging in *satyagraha* and experiencing suffering on behalf of justice, purifies the soul from pollution emanating from man's animal nature:

> A *satyagrahi* is dead to his body even before his enemy attempts to kill him, i.e. he is free from the attachments of his body and lives only in the victory of his soul. (*Nonviolence in Peace and War*, I, p. 318) Nonviolence implies as complete self-purification as is humanly possible. (*Nonviolence in Peace and War*, I, p. 111)

By acting nonviolently, pacifists not only purify their own souls but also transform the souls of their opponents: "A nonviolent revolution is not a program of seizure of power. It is a program of transformation of relationships, ending in peaceful transfer of power" (*Nonviolence in Peace and War*, II, p. 8)

Though in most places Gandhi emphasizes the personal redemption that is possible only through nonviolent resistance to evil, the spiritually positive effect of nonviolence on evil opponents is perhaps equally important, since "The sword of the *satyagrahi* is love" (*Nonviolence in Peace and War*, II, p. 59).

Gandhi, then, is far from preaching the sacredness of biological life. What matters is not biological life but the condition of the soul, the natural and proper state of which is *ahimsa*. The evil of violence is that it distorts and disrupts this natural condition of the soul. The basic moral law (*dharma*) for all people is to seek the restoration of their souls to the harmony of *ahimsa*. This spiritual restoration cannot be achieved by violence, but only by the application of *satyagraha*. Disharmony cannot produce harmony; violence cannot produce spiritual peace.

The "sacredness of life" defense of pacifism ran into difficulties analyzing situations in which taking one life could save many lives. For Gandhi, this is no problem at all: taking one life may save many biological lives, but it will not save souls. On the contrary, the soul of the killer will be perverted by the act, and that perversion—not loss of life—is what matters morally.

The system of values professed by Gandhi—that the highest human good is a harmonious condition of soul—must be kept in mind when considering the frequent accusation that Gandhi's method of nonviolent resistance "does not work," that nonviolence alone did not and could not force the British to leave India, and that nonviolent resistance to murderous tyrants like Hitler will only provoke the mass murder of the innocent. Perhaps the practice of nonviolence could not "defeat" the British or "defeat" Hitler, but by Gandhi's standards the use of military force would only produce a greater defeat, perverting the souls of thousands engaged in war and intensifying the will to violence on the opposing side. On the other hand, the soul of the *satyagrahi* will be strengthened and purified by nonviolent struggle against British imperialism or German Nazism, and in this purification the Gandhian pacifist can obtain spiritual victory even in the face of political defeat.

India did not adopt the creed of nonviolence after the British left in 1948, and it is hardly likely that any modern nation-state will organize its international affairs along Gandhian lines. But none of this affects the validity of Gandhi's arguments, which indicate how things ought to be, not how they are. We have seen that Gandhi's principles do not falter in the face of situations in which taking one life can save lives on balance. But what of situations in which the sacrifice of spiritual purity by one will prevent the corruption of many souls? Suppose, for example, that a Gandhian believes (on good evidence) that a well-timed commando raid will prevent a nation from embarking on an aggressive war, a war that would inflame whole populations with hatred for the enemy. Wouldn't a concern with one's own spiritual purity in such a situation show an immoral lack of concern for the souls of one's fellow men?

Another problem for Gandhi concerns the relationship between violence and coercion. To coerce people is to make them act against their will, for fear of the consequences they will suffer if they do not obey. Coercion, then, is a kind of spiritual violence, directed against the imagination and will of the victim. The "violence" most conspicuously rejected by Gandhi— pushing, shoving, striking with hands, the use of weapons, the placing of bombs and explosives—is essentially physical violence, directed against the bodies of opponents. But if physical violence against bodies is spiritually corrupting, psychological violence directed at the will of opponents must be even more corrupting.

In his writings Gandhi condemned coercion. Yet in practice he can hardly be said to have renounced *psychological* coercion. Obviously he would have preferred to have the British depart from India of their own free will, deciding that it was in their own best interest, or at least morally necessary, to leave. But if the British had decided, in the absence of coercion, to stay, Gandhi was prepared to exert every kind of nonviolent pressure to make them go. And when Gandhi on occasion attempted to achieve political objectives by a "fast unto death," his threat of self-starvation brought enormous psychological pressure on the authorities, who, among other things, feared the riots that would ensue should Gandhi die.

The Gandhian pacifist, then, must explain why psychological pressure is permissible if physical pressure is forbidden. One possible answer is that physical pressure cannot transform the soul of the opponents, but psychological pressure, since it operates on the mind, can effect a spiritual transformation. Indeed, Gandhi characterized his terrifying fasts as acts of education, not coercion. But the claim that these fasts were not coercive confuses the noncoercive intention behind the act with its predictable coercive effects; and if education is the name of the game, the nonpacifist will remark that violence has been known to teach a few good lessons in its day.

In many spiritual traditions, what matters essentially is not the kind of pressure but that the right pressure be applied at the right time and in the right way. Zen masters have brought students to enlightenment by clouting them on the ears, and God helped St. Paul to see the light by knocking him off his horse.

In addition to these technical problems, many people will be inclined to reject the system of values from which Gandhi's deductions flow. Many will concede that good character is important and that helping others to develop moral virtues is an important task. But few agree with Gandhi that the development of moral purity is the supreme human good, and that other goods, like the preservation of human life, or progress in the arts and sciences, have little or no value in comparison. If even a little value is conceded to these other things, then on occasion it will be necessary to put aside the project of developing spiritual purity in order to preserve other values. These acts of preservation may require physical violence, and those who use violence to defend life or beauty or liberty may indeed be corrupting their souls. But it is hard to believe that an occasional and necessary act of violence on behalf of these values will totally and permanently corrupt the soul, and those who use violence judiciously may be right in thinking that the saving of life or beauty or liberty may be worth a small or temporary spiritual loss.

4. PRIVATE PACIFISM

Perhaps the rarest form of pacifist is the pacifist who renounces violence in personal relations but condones the use of force in the political sphere. Such a pacifist will not use violence for self-defense but believes that it is permissible for the state to use judicial force against criminals and military force against foreign enemies. A private pacifist renounces self-defense but supports national defense.

(a) Augustine's Limited Pacifism

Historically, private pacifism developed as an attempt to reconcile the demands of the Sermon on the Mount with the Christian duty of charity. The Sermon on the Mount requires Christians to "resist not evil"; the duty of charity requires pity for the weak who suffer the injustice of the strong. For St. Augustine (354–430), one essential message of the Gospels is the good news that this present life is as nothing compared with the life to come. The person who tries to hold on to earthly possessions is deluded as to what is truly valuable: "If any man will sue thee at the law, and take away thy coat, let him have thy cloak also" (Matt. 5:40). What goes for earthly coats should go for earthly life as well, so if any man seeks to take a Christian life, the Christian should let him have it. On this view, the doc-

trine "resist not evil" is just an expression of contempt for earthly possessions.

But according to Augustine there are some things in this world that
do have value: justice, for example, the relief of suffering, and the preservation of the Church, which Augustine equated with civilization itself. To
defend these things with necessary force is not to fall prey to delusions
about the good. For Augustine, then, service in the armed forces is not
inconsistent with Christian values.

One difficulty for theories like Augustine's is that they seem to justify
military service only when military force is used in a just cause. Unfor-
tunately, once in the service, the man in the ranks is not in a position to
evaluate the justice of his nation's cause; indeed, in many modern nations,
the principle of military subordination to civilian rule prevents even generals from evaluating the purposes of war declared by political leaders. But
Augustine argues that the cause of justice cannot be served without armies,
and armies cannot function unless subordinates follow orders without
questioning the purposes of the conflict. The necessary conditions for justice and charity require that some men put themselves in positions in which
they might be required to fight for injustice.

(b) The Problem of Self-Defense

Many will agree with Augustine that most violence at the personal
level—the violence of crime, vendetta, and domestic brutality, for example—goes contrary to moral principles. But most are prepared to draw the
line at personal and collective self-defense. Can the obligation to be charitable justify participation in military service but stop short of justifying the
use of force by private citizens, if that force is exercised to protect the weak
from the oppression of the strong? Furthermore, the obligation to be charitable does not exclude acts of charity toward oneself. For Augustine, violence was a dangerous tool, best kept out of the hands of the citizens and
best left strictly at the disposal of the state. Beset with fears of crime in the
streets, the contemporary American is less inclined to worry about the
anarchic effects of private uses of defensive force and more inclined to
worry about the protection the police seem unable to provide.

For these worried people, the existence of a right to self-defense is
self-evident. But the existence of this right is not self-evident to universal or
private pacifists, and it was not self-evident to St. Augustine. In the Christian tradition, no right to self-defense was recognized until its existence was
certified by Thomas Aquinas in the thirteenth century. Aquinas derived
the right to self-defense from the universal tendency to self-preservation,
assuming (contrary to Augustine) that a natural tendency must be morally
right. As for the Christian duty to love one's enemy, Aquinas argued that
acts of self-defense have two effects—the saving of life and the taking of
life—and that self-defensive uses of force intend primarily the saving of

life. This makes the use of force in self-defense a morally permissible act of charity. The right to self-defense is now generally recognized in Catholic moral theology and in Western legal systems. But it can hardly be said that Aquinas's arguments, which rely heavily on assumptions from Greek philosophy, succeed in reconciling the claims of self-defense with the prescriptions of the Sermon on the Mount.

5. ANTIWAR PACIFISM

Most people who believe in the right to personal self-defense also believe that some wars are morally justified. In fact, the notion of self-defense and the notion of just war are commonly linked: just wars are said to be defensive wars, and the justice of defensive war is inferred from the right of personal self-defense, projected from the individual to the national level. But some people reject this projection: they endorse the validity of personal self-defense, but they deny that war can be justified by appeal to self-defense or any other right. On the contrary, they argue that war always involves an inexcusable violation of rights. For such anti-war pacifists, all participation in war is morally wrong.

(a) The Killing of Soldiers

One universal and necessary feature of wars is that soldiers get killed in them. Most people accept such killings as a necessary evil, and judge the killing of soldiers in war to be morally acceptable. If the war is fought for a just cause, the killing of enemy soldiers is justified as necessary to the triumph of right. If the war is fought for an unjust cause, the killing of enemy soldiers is acceptable because it is considered an honorable thing to fight for one's country, right or wrong, provided that one fights well and cleanly. But the antiwar pacifist does not take the killing of soldiers for granted. Everyone has a right to life, and the killing of soldiers in war is intentional killing, a deliberate violation of the right to life. According to the standard interpretation of basic rights, it is never morally justifiable to violate a basic right in order to produce some good; the end, in such cases, does not justify the means. How, then, can the killing of soldiers in war be morally justified—or even excused?

Perhaps the commonest reply to the challenge of antiwar pacifism is that killing in war is a matter of self-defense, *personal* self-defense, the right to which is freely acknowledged by the antiwar pacifist. In war, the argument goes, it is either kill or be killed—and that type of killing is killing in self-defense. But though the appeal to self-defense is natural, antiwar pacifists believe that it is not successful. First of all, on the usual understanding of "self-defense," those who kill can claim the justification of self-defense only if (a) they had no other way to save their lives or preserve themselves from physical harm except by killing, and (b) they did nothing to provoke the attack to which they are subjected. Antiwar pacifists point out that soldiers on the battlefield do have a way of saving themselves from death or harm without killing anyone: they can surrender. Furthermore, for soldiers fighting for an unjust cause—for example, German soldiers fighting in the invasion of Russia in 1941—it is difficult to argue that they "did nothing to provoke" the deadly force directed at them. But if the German army provoked the Russians to stand and fight on Russian soil, German soldiers cannot legitimately claim self-defense as a moral justification for killing Russian soldiers.

To the nonpacifist, these points might seem like legalistic quibbles. But the antiwar pacifist has an even stronger argument against killing soldiers in war. The vast majority of soldiers who die in war do not die in "kill or be killed" situations. They are killed by bullets, shells, or bombs directed from safe launching points—"safe" in the sense that those who shoot the bullets or fire the shells or drop the bombs are in no immediate danger of death. Since those who kill are not in immediate danger of death, they cannot invoke "self-defense" to justify the deaths they cause.

Some other argument besides self-defense, then, must explain why the killing of soldiers in war should not be classified as murder. Frequently, nonpacifists argue that the explanation is found in the doctrine of "assumption of risk," the idea, common in civil law, that persons who freely assume a risk have only themselves to blame if the risk is realized. When a soldier goes to war, he is well aware that one risk of his trade is getting killed on the battlefield. If he dies on the field, the responsibility for his death lies with himself, not with the man who shot him. By assuming the risk—so the argument goes—he waived his right to life, at least on the battlefield.

One does not have to be a pacifist to see difficulties in this argument. First of all, in all substantial modern wars, most of the men on the line are not volunteers, but draftees. Only a wealthy nation like the United States can afford an all-volunteer army, and most experts believe that the American volunteer ranks will have to be supplemented by draftees should the United States become involved in another conflict on the scale of Korea or Vietnam. Second, in many cases in which a risk is realized, responsibility for the bad outcome lies not with the person who assumed the risk but with the person who created it. If an arsonist sets fire to a house and a parent rushes in to save the children, dying in the rescue attempt, responsibility for the parent's death lies not with the parent who assumed the risk but with the arsonist who created it. So if German armies invade Russia, posing the risk of death in battle, and if Russian soldiers assume this risk and fight back, the deaths of Russians are the fault of German invaders, not the fault of the defenders who assumed the risk.

These criticisms of German foot soldiers will irritate many who served in the armed forces and who know how little political and military decision making is left to the men on the front lines, who seem to be the special target of these pacifist arguments. But antiwar pacifists will deny that their aim is to condemn the men on the battlefield. Most antiwar pacifists feel that soldiers in war act under considerable compulsion and are excused for that reason from responsibility for the killing they do. But to say that battlefield killings are *excusable* is not to say that they are morally *justified*. On the contrary, if such killings are excusable, it must be that there is some immorality to be excused.

(b) The Killing of Civilians

In the chronicles of ancient wars, conflict was total and loss in battle was frequently followed by general slaughter of men, women, and children on the losing side. It has always been considered part of the trend toward civilization to confine the destruction of war to the personnel and instruments of war, sparing civilians and their property as much as possible. This civilizing trend was conspicuously reversed in World War II, in which the ratio of civilian deaths to total war deaths was perhaps the highest it had been since the wars of religion in the seventeenth century. A very high ratio of civilian deaths to total deaths was also characteristic of the war in Vietnam. Given the immense firepower of modern weapons and the great distances between the discharges of weapons and the explosions of bullets or shells near the targets, substantial civilian casualties are an inevitable part of modern land war. But it is immoral to kill civilians, the antiwar pacifist argues, and from this it follows that modern land warfare is necessarily immoral.

Few nonpacifists will argue that killing enemy civilians is justifiable when such killings are avoidable. Few will argue that killing enemy civilians is justifiable when such killings are the *primary* objective of a military operation. But what about the deaths of civilians that are the unavoidable results of military operations directed to some *other* result? The pacifist classifies such killings as immoral, whereas most nonpacifists call them regrettable but unavoidable deaths, not murders. But why are they not murder, if the civilians are innocent, and if it is known in advance that some civilians will be killed? Isn't this an intentional killing of the innocent, which is the traditional definition of murder?

The sophisticated nonpacifist may try to parry this thrust with analogies to policies outside the arena of war. There are, after all, many morally acceptable policies that, when adopted, have the effect of killing innocent persons. If the Congress decides to set a speed limit of 55 miles per hour on federal highways, more people will die than if Congress sets the speed limit at 45 miles per hour. Since many people who die on the highway are innocent, the Congress has chosen a policy that knowingly brings death to the innocent, but no one calls it murder. Or suppose, for example, that a public health officer is considering a national vaccination program to forestall a flu epidemic. He knows that if he does not implement the vaccination program, many people will die from the flu. On the other hand, if the program is implemented, a certain number of people will die from allergic reactions to the vaccine. Most of the people who die from allergic reactions will be people who would not have died of the flu if the vaccination program had not been implemented. So the vaccination program will kill innocent people who would otherwise be saved if the program were abandoned. If the public health officer implements such a program, we do *not* think that he is a murderer.

Nonpacifists argue that what makes the action of Congress and the action of the public health officer morally permissible in these cases is that the deaths of the innocent, although foreseen, are not the intended goal of these policies. Congress does not want people to die on the highways; every highway death is a regrettable death. The purpose of setting the speed limit at 55 miles per hour is not to kill people but to provide a reasonable balance between safety and convenience. Likewise, it is not the purpose of the public health officer to kill people by giving them vaccine. His goal is to save lives on balance, and every death from the vaccine is a regrettable death. Likewise, in war, when civilians are killed as a result of necessary military operations, the deaths of the civilians are not the intended goal of the military operation. They are foreseen, but they are always regretted. If we do not accuse the Congress of murder and the Public Health Service of murder in these cases, consistency requires that we not accuse military forces of murder when they cause civilian deaths in war, especially if every attempt is made to keep civilian deaths to a minimum.

Antiwar pacifists do not condemn the Congress and the Public Health Service in cases like these. But they assert that the case of war is different in a morally relevant way. To demonstrate the difference, antiwar pacifists provide an entirely different analysis of the moral justification for speed limits and vaccination programs. In their opinion, the facts that highway deaths and vaccination deaths are "unintended" and "regretted" is morally irrelevant. The real justification lies in the factor of consent. In the case of federal highway regulations, the rules are decided by Congress, which is elected by the people, the same people who use the highways. If Congress decides on a 55-mile-an-hour speed limit, this is a regulation that, in some sense, highway drivers have imposed upon themselves. Those people who die on the highway because of a higher speed limit have, in a double sense, assumed the risks generated by that speed limit: they have, through the Congress, created the risk, and by venturing onto the highway, have freely exposed themselves to the risk. The responsibility for these highway deaths, then, lies either on the drivers themselves or on the people who crashed into them—not on the Congress.

Likewise, in the case of the vaccination program, if people are warned in advance of the risks of vaccination, and if they nevertheless choose to be vaccinated, they are responsible for their own deaths should the risks be realized. According to the antiwar pacifist, it is this consent given by drivers and vaccination volunteers that justifies these policies, and it is precisely this element of consent that is absent in the case of the risks inflicted on enemy civilians in time of war.

Consider the standard textbook example of allegedly justifiable killing of civilians in time of war. Suppose that the destruction of a certain bridge is an important military objective, but if the bridge is bombed, it is very likely that civilians living close by will be killed. (The civilians cannot be warned without alerting the enemy to reinforce the bridge.) If the bridge is bombed and some civilians are killed, the bombing victims are not in the same moral category as highway victims or victims of vaccination. The bombing victims did not order the bombing of themselves through some set of elected representatives. Nor did the bombing victims freely consent to the bombing of their bridge. Nor was the bombing in any way undertaken as a calculated risk in the interest of the victims. For all these reasons, the moral conclusions regarding highway legislation and vaccination programs do not carry over to bombing of the bridge.

Nonpacifists who recognize that it will be very difficult to fight wars without bombing bridges may argue that the victims of this bombing in some sense assumed the risks of bombardment by choosing to live close to a potential military target. Indeed, it is occasionally claimed that all the civilians in a nation at war have assumed the risks of war, since they could avoid the risks of war simply by moving to a neutral country. But such arguments are strained and uncharitable, even for those rare warring nations that permit freedom of emigration. Most people consider it a major sacrifice to give up their homes, and an option that requires such a sacrifice cannot be considered an option open for free choice. The analogy between the unintended victims of vaccination and the unintended civilian victims of war seems to have broken down.

(c)　The Balance of Good and Evil in War

It is left to the nonpacifist to argue that the killing of soldiers and civilians in war is in the end justifiable in order to obtain great moral goods that can be obtained only by fighting for them. Civilians have rights to life, but those rights can be outweighed by the national objectives, provided those objectives are morally acceptable and overwhelmingly important. Admittedly, this argument for killing civilians is available only to the just side in a war, but if the argument is valid, it proves that there can *be* a just side, contrary to the arguments of antiwar pacifism.

Antiwar pacifists have two lines of defense. First, they can continue to maintain that the end does not justify the means, if the means be murderous. Second, they can, and will, go on to argue that it is a tragic mistake to believe that there are great moral goods that can be obtained only by war. According to antiwar pacifists, the amount of moral good produced by war is greatly exaggerated. The Mexican War, for example, resulted in half of Mexico being transferred to American rule. This was a great good for the United States, but not a great moral good, since the United States had little claim to the ceded territory, and no great injustice would have persisted if the war had not been fought at all.

The Revolutionary War in America is widely viewed as a war that produced a great moral good; but if the war had not been fought, the history of the United States would be similar to the history of Canada (which remained loyal)—and no one feels that the Canadians have suffered or are suffering great injustices that the American colonies avoided by war. Likewise, it is difficult to establish the goods produced by World War I or the moral losses that would have ensued if the winning side, "our side," had lost. Bertrand Russell imagined the results of a British loss in World War I as follows:

> The greatest sum that foreigners could possibly exact would be the total economic rent of the land and natural resources of England. [But] the working classes, the shopkeepers, manufacturers, and merchants, the literary men and men of science—all the people that make England of any account in the world—have at most an infinitesimal and accidental share in the rental of England. The men who have a share use their rents in luxury, political corruption, taking the lives of birds, and depopulating and enslaving the rural districts. It is this life of the idle rich that would be curtailed if the Germans exacted tribute from England. (*Justice in War Time*, pp. 48–49)

But multiplying examples of wars that did little moral good will not establish the pacifist case. The pacifist must show that *no* war has done enough good to justify the killing of soldiers and the killing of civilians that occurred in the war. A single war that produces moral goods sufficient to justify its killings will refute the pacifist claim that *all* wars are morally unjustifiable. Obviously this brings the antiwar pacifist head to head with World War II.

It is commonly estimated that 35 million people died as a result of World War II. It is difficult to imagine that any cause could justify so much death, but fortunately the Allies need only justify their share of these killings. Between 1939 and 1945 Allied forces killed about 5.5 million Axis soldiers and about 1 million civilians in Axis countries. Suppose that Britain and the United States had chosen to stay out of World War II and suppose that Stalin had, like Lenin, surrendered to Germany shortly after the invasion. Does avoiding the world that would have resulted from these decisions justify killing 6.5 million people?

If Hitler and Tojo had won the war, doubtless they would have killed a great many people both before and after victory, but it is quite likely that the total of *additional* victims, beyond those they killed in the war that *was* fought, would have been less than 6.5 million and, at any rate, the responsibility for those deaths would fall on Hitler and Tojo, not on Allied nations.

If Hitler and Tojo had won the war, large portions of the world would have fallen under foreign domination, perhaps for a very long time. But the antiwar pacifist will point out that the main areas of Axis foreign domination—China and Russia—were not places in which the citizens enjoyed a high level of freedom *before the war began*. Perhaps the majority of people in the conquered areas would have worked out a *modus vivendi* with their new rulers, as did the majority of French citizens during the German occupation. Nor can it be argued that World War II was necessary to save six million Jews from annihilation in the Holocaust, since in fact the war did *not* save them.

The ultimate aims of Axis leaders are a matter for historical debate. Clearly the Japanese had no intention of conquering the United States, and some historians suggest that Hitler hoped to avoid war with England and America, declaring war with England reluctantly, and only after the English declared it against him. Nevertheless, popular opinion holds that Hitler intended to conquer the world, and if preventing the conquest of Russia and China could not justify six and one-half million killings, most Americans are quite confident that preventing the conquest of England and the United States does justify killing on this scale.

The anitwar pacifist disagrees. Certainly German rule of England and the United States would have been a very bad thing. At the same time, hatred of such German rule would be partially fueled by hatred of foreigners, and hatred of foreigners, as such, is an irrational and morally unjustifiable passion. After all, if rule by foreigners were, by itself, a great moral wrong, the British, with their great colonial empire, could hardly consider themselves the morally superior side in World War II.

No one denies that a Nazi victory in World War II would have had morally frightful results. But, according to antiwar pacifism, killing six and one-half million people is also morally frightful, and preventing one moral wrong does not obviously outweigh committing the other. Very few people today share the pacifists' condemnation of World War II, but perhaps that is because the dead killed by the Allies cannot speak up and make sure that their losses are properly counted on the moral scales. Antiwar pacifists speak on behalf of the enemy dead, and on behalf of all those millions who would have lived if the war had not been fought. On this silent constituency they rest their moral case.

6. SUGGESTIONS FOR FURTHER READING

Varieties of Pacifism

For histories of pacifism that capture the variety of the subject, see the following works of Peter Brock: *Pacifism in the U.S. from the Colonial Era to the 18th Century* (Princeton, NJ: Princeton University Press, 1968); *Pacifism in Europe to 1914* (Princeton, NJ: Princeton University Press, 1972); and *Twentieth Century Pacifism* (New York: Van Nostrand, 1976). A recent book sensitive to the variety of pacifisms is Jenny Teichman, *Pacifism and the Just War* (New York: Basil Blackwell, 1986).

The Prohibition Against Killing

For a recent discussion of pacifism vs. divine crusade in the Hebrew Bible, see Paul D. Hanson, "War and Peace in the Hebrew Bible," *Interpretation* (October 1984).

For arguments that the sacredness of life leads to an absolute ban on taking life, see Albert Schweitzer, *The Teaching of Reverence for Life*, trans. Richard and Clara Masters (New York: Holt, Rinehart, Winston, 1965).

The argument that commitment to a right to life does not imply pacifism is developed by Jan Narveson in "Pacifism, A Philosophical Analysis," in *War and Morality*, ed. Richard Wasserstrom (Belmont, CA: Wadsworth, 1970)

Universal Pacifism

A classic account of pacifism in early Christianity and its dissipation is Adolph Harnack, *Militia Christi*, trans. David McI. Gracie (Philadelphia: Fortress Press, 1981). See also C. John Cadoux, *The Early Christian Attitude to War* (New York: Seabury Press, 1982); R. H. Bainton, *Christian Attitudes Towards War and Peace* (Nashville, TN: Abingdon Press, 1960); F. H. Russell, *The Just War in the Middle Ages* (New York: Cambridge University Press, 1975); and Victor P. Furnish, "War and Peace in the New Testament," *Interpretation* (October 1984).

Two contemporary Christian sects that endorse pacifism are the Quakers and the Mennonites. On Quaker pacifism, see E. V. B. Foulds, *The Story of Quakerism* (Richmond, IN: Friends United Press, 1967) and *Quaker Spirituality*, ed. Douglas Steere (New York: Paulist Press, 1984). On Mennonite pacifism, see John H. Yoder, *What Would You Do?* (Scottsdale, PA: Herald Press, 1973) and *When War Is Unjust: Being Honest in Just War Thinking* (Minneapolis: Augsburg, 1984).

Tolstoy's "moral exemplar" argument is found in *My Religion*, Chapters 4 and 6, in *The Collected Works of Count Lev N. Tolstoy*, trans. Leo Wiener (New York: John Wanamaker, 1904). Also important for Tolstoy's pacifism are his *The Kingdom of God Is Within You, or, Christianity not as a Mystical Teaching but as a New Concept of Life*, trans. Leo Wiener (New York: Farrar, Straus, Giroux, 1961), and his *The Law of Love and the Law of Violence*, trans. Mary Koutouzow Tolstoy (New York: Holt, Rinehart, and Winston, 1971).

Gandhi's thoughts on nonviolence are scattered throughout the hundred or more volumes of his collected works. His pronouncements on specific wars and military events are collected in *Nonviolence in Peace and War*, ed. Mahadev Desai, 2 vols. (Ahmedabad: Navajivan Press, 1945, repr. 1960). The metaphysical background of Gandhi's thinking is described in William Borman, *Gandhi and Nonviolence* (Buffalo: State University of New York Press, 1986). Perhaps the most complete discussion of Gandhian methods and politics is Gene Sharp, *The Politics of Nonviolent Action*, 3 vols. (Boston: Porter Sargent, 1973).

Private Pacifism

Augustine's thoughts on war and self-defense are expounded in his *On the Freedom of the Will*, I, v. See also the section on just war in *The Political Writings of St. Augustine*, ed. Henry Paolucci (Chicago: Regnery, 1962). For analysis of Augustine's views, see Paul Ramsey, *War and the Christian Conscience* (Durham, NC: Duke University Press, 1961); and F. van der Meer, *Augustine the Bishop* (New York: Harper and Row, 1961).

Aquinas' discussion of self-defense is in the *Summa Theolgiae*, II-II, 64.

For contemporary philosophical analyses of the concept of self-defense, see Judith Thomson, "Self-Defense and Rights" (1976), in *Rights, Restitution, and Risk* (Cambridge, MA: Harvard University Press, 1985); Jeffrey Blustein, "Proportionality and the Psychotic Aggressor," *Ottawa Law Review* 10 (1978); and C. C. Ryan, "Self-Defense and the Possibility of Killing," *Ethics* (April 1983).

Antiwar Pacifism

An interesting discussion of how soldiers lose the standard right to life is in Michael Walzer, *Just and Unjust Wars* (New York: Basic Books, 1977). Walzer argues that the "war convention" trades the soldier's right to life for the rights of war, such as the right to be respected as a prisoner of war. For criticism, see Douglas Lackey, "A Modern Theory of Just War," *Ethics* (April 1982).

The argument that the deaths of civilians in war are morally justifiable, provided those deaths are not directly intended, assumes the moral significance of "foreseen" vs. "intended" deaths, usually called the "principle of double effect." For a history of this principle, see T. Mangan, "A Historical Analysis of the Principle of Double Effect," *Theological Studies* 19 (1949). Perhaps the most spirited modern defense of the principle is G. E. M. Anscombe's "War and Murder" (1961) in *Moral Problems*, ed. James Rachels, 3rd ed. (New York: Harper and Row, 1982); see also Philip Devine, *The Ethics of Homicide* (Ithaca, NY: Cornell University Press, 1978); and Charles Fried, *Right and Wrong* (Cambridge, MA: Harvard University Press, 1978). For attacks on the principle, see Philippa Foot, "The Problem of Abortion and the Principle of Double Effect" (1967) in *Moral Problems*;

Jonathan Bennett, "Morality and Consequences," in *Tanner Lectures on Human Values*, II, ed. Sterling McMurrin (Cambridge: Cambridge University Press, 1981); and Douglas Lackey, "The Moral Irrelevance of the Counterforce/Countervalue Distinction," *The Monist* (July 1987).

The idea that there are "innocent civilians" in a country at war is attacked by James Child, "Political Responsibility and NonCombatant Liability," in *Political Realism and International Morality*, ed. Kenneth Kipnis and Diana Meyers (Boulder, CO: Westview Press, 1987). Gertrude Ezorsky argues in "War and Innocence," *Public Affairs Quarterly* (April 1987), that it is always morally wrong to kill children, directly or indirectly, which implies that most wars cannot be morally undertaken.

The Balance of Good and Evil in War

The classic argument that wars are not worth the effort is Norman Angell, *The Great Illusion: A Study of the Relation of Military Power in Nations to the Economic and Social Advantage* (London: Putnam's, 1912). See also Donald A. Wells, *The War Myth* (New York: Pegasus, 1967). For an analytical review of the evils perpetrated by the Nazis see Douglas Lackey, "Extraordinary Evil or Common Malevolence? Evaluating the Jewish Holocaust," *Journal of Applied Philosophy* 3.2 (1987).

3
JUST WAR THEORY I

When to Fight

1. INTRODUCTION

Rightly or wrongly, pacifism has always been a minority view. Most people believe that *some* wars are morally justifiable; the majority of Americans believe that World War II was a moral war. But though most people have clear-cut intuitions about the moral acceptability of World War II, the Vietnam War, and so forth, few people have a theory that justifies and organizes their intuitive judgments. If morally concerned nonpacifists are to defeat the pacifists to their moral left and the cynics to their moral right, they must develop a theory that will distinguish justifiable wars from unjustifiable wars, using a set of consistent and consistently applied rules.

The work of specifying these rules, which dates at least from Aristotle's *Politics*, traditionally goes under the heading of "just war theory." The name is slightly misleading, since justice is only one of several primary moral concepts, all of which must be consulted in a complete moral evaluation of war. A just war—a morally good war—is not merely a war dictated by principles of justice. A just war is a morally justifiable war after justice, human rights, the common good, and all other relevant moral concepts have been consulted and weighed against the facts and against each other.

Just war theorists sometimes fail to notice that just war theory describes two sorts of just wars: wars that are morally permissible and wars that are morally obligatory. The distinction between the permissible and the obligatory is persuasively demonstrable at the personal level. If I am unjustly attacked, I have a right to use force in my own defense—assuming that I have no other recourse. But since it is always open for the holder of a right to waive that right, I am not *obliged* to use force in my own defense. But suppose that I have promised to defend Jones, that Jones is now exposed to unjust attack, and that Jones calls for my help. In such a case I am obliged to defend Jones. At the level of nations, the distinction between permissible war and obligatory war has important consequences for policy. Frequently policy analysts demonstrate that a certain use of force passes the tests of just war, and then infer that the war is obligatory, that "justice demands it." But it may well be that the use of force is merely permissible, in which case it is also permissible to forgo the use of force. Indeed, there may be powerful prudential considerations why such a merely permissible just war should not be fought.

Another little point in the logic of just war theory deserves attention. In just war theory, the terms "just" and "unjust" are logical contraries. It follows that in war one side at most can be the just side. But it is possible that both sides may be unjust, and it is fallacious to think that if one side is provably unjust, the other side must be provably just. If your enemy is evil, it does not follow that you are good.

In undertaking the moral evaluation of war, it is natural to distinguish rules that determine *when* it is permissible or obligatory to begin a war (*jus ad bellum*) from rules that determine *how* a war should be fought once it has begun (*jus in bello*). *Jus ad bellum* rules apply principally to political leaders; *jus in bello* rules apply principally to soldiers and their officers. The distinction is not ironclad, since there may be situations in which there is no morally permissible way to wage war, in which case it follows that the war should not be waged in the first place. (Some believe that American intervention in Vietnam was such a case.) In this chapter we take up *jus ad bellum*; Chapter 4 is devoted to *jus in bello*.

2.   COMPETENT AUTHORITY

From the time of Augustine, theorists have maintained that a just war can be prosecuted only by a "competent authority." Augustine, as we noted, considered the use of force by private persons to be immoral; consequently the only permissible uses of force were those sanctioned by public authorities. Medieval authors, with a watchful eye for peasant revolts, followed Augustine in confining the just use of force to princes, whose authority and patronage were divinely sanctioned. Given these scholastic roots, considerations of competent authority might appear archaic, but it is still helpful for purposes of moral judgment to distinguish wars from spontaneous uprisings, and soldiers and officers from pirates and brigands. Just war must, first of all, be war.

To begin, most scholars agree that war is a controlled use of force, undertaken by persons organized in a functioning chain of command. An isolated assassin cannot wage war; New York City's Mad Bomber in the 1950s only metaphorically waged war against Con Edison. In some sense, then, war is the contrary of violence. Second, the use of force in war must be directed to an identifiable political result, a requirement forever associated with the Prussian theorist Karl von Clauswitz. An "identifiable political result" is some change in a government's policy, some alteration in a form of government, or some extension or limitation of the scope of its authority. Since the extermination of a people is not an identifiable political result, most acts of genocide are not acts of war: the Turks did not wage war against the Armenians, nor did Hitler wage war on the Jews. (The American frontier cliché, "the only good Indian is a dead Indian" expresses the hopes of murderers, not soldiers.) And since the religious conversion of people is, in most cases, not a political result, many holy wars, by this definition, have not been wars.

Our definition of war as the controlled use of force for political purposes does not imply that wars can be waged only by the governments of nation-states. Many rebels and revolutionaries have used controlled force through a chain of command for political purposes, and there have been at least as many wars within states as there have been wars between states. If civil wars are genuine wars, the scope of "competent authority" must be extended from princes and political leaders to rebels and revolutionaries as well. But, as the case of Pancho Villa perhaps indicates, it is sometimes difficult to distinguish revolutionaries from bandits. In international law, this difficulty is described as the problem of determining when a rebel movement has obtained "belligerent status."

In the most recent international discussion of this issue, at the Geneva Conference of 1974–1977, delegates agreed that in the case of conflicts arising within a single nation-state between the government and "dissident armed forces or other organized groups," a state of war shall exist, provided the dissident forces are

> . . . under responsible command, exercise such control over part of its territory as to enable them to carry out sustained and concerted military operations and [to implement the laws of war]. (Protocol II, Article 1.1)

This recognition of belligerent status, however,

> shall not apply to situations of internal disturbances and tensions, such as riots, isolated and sporadic acts of violence, and other acts of similar nature, as not being armed conflicts. (Protocol I, Article 1.2)

According to these rules, the American Confederacy in 1860, by virtue of its military organization and control of territory, qualifies for belligerent status, whereas the Symbionese Liberation Army, which controlled no territory, and the Newark rioters of 1967, who obeyed no commands, fail to qualify. By this standard, the American Civil War was war but the Patty Hearst kidnapping was crime, verdicts with which most people would agree.

But the new Geneva standard does not always yield satisfactory results. The partisan movements in World War II—the resistance movements in France, Italy, and the Ukraine, and Tito's great movement in Yugoslavia—rarely could claim specific territory as their own, yet their struggles can hardly be dismissed as unjust on grounds of absence of competent authority. Different perplexities arise in the case of peasant movements, where frequently territory is controlled from the capital by day and by the revolutionaries at night. Perhaps the requirement of "territorial control" is too strong.

The new Geneva standard also requires that genuine belligerents must be capable of carrying out "sustained and concerted military operations." This proviso would deny belligerent status to revolutionary groups that engage primarily in terrorist attacks against civilians, and most people would happily classify such terrorists as international outlaws. But what of revolutionary groups that do not engage in "sustained and concerted military operations"—which, in many cases, would be suicidal for the revolutionaries—but engage in sustained acts of terror against government buildings and officials of the incumbent regime? The campaign of assassination directed by the National Liberation Front (NLF) in Vietnam against village chiefs and other officials siding with the Saigon government was, at one point, the main form of its revolutionary struggle, and it seems pointless to deny the NLF belligerent status on the ground that its members were not engaging in sustained and concerted military operations. Though it might be criticized on other grounds, the NLF assassination campaign was controlled use of force directed to political ends, not a riot and not sporadic violence. It was dirty, but it was war.

3. RIGHT INTENTION

One can imagine cases in which a use of military force might satisfy all the external standards of just war while those who order this use of force have no concern for justice. Unpopular political leaders, for example, might choose to make war in order to stifle domestic dissent and win the next election. The traditional theory of just war insists that a just war be a war for the right, fought for the sake of the right.

In the modern climate of political realism, many authors are inclined to treat the standard of right intention as a quaint relic of a more idealistic age, either on the grounds that moral motives produce disastrous results in international politics or on the grounds that motives are subjective and unobservable. ("I will not speculate on the motives of the North Vietnamese," Henry Kissinger once remarked, "I have too much difficulty understanding our own.") But it is unfair to dismiss idealistic motives on the grounds that they produce disaster in international politics, since realistic motives have produced their own fair share of disasters. It is a mistake to dismiss motives as unobservable, when they are so often clearly exhibited in behavior. The real difficulty with the demand for idealistic motives is that people usually have more than one motive for each of their actions, which makes it difficult or impossible to specify *the* motive for the act.

Despite the difficulty of multiple motives, it is important to retain some version of the rule of right intention as part of the theory of just war. No thoughtful person can fail to be disturbed by current international practice, in which leaders make policy decisions without regard for moral considerations and then have their staffs cook up moral rationalizations after the fact. If it is too much to insist that political leaders take decisions solely on moral grounds or even primarily on moral grounds, we can insist that desire for what is morally right be at least *one* of their motives.

It follows from this qualified insistence on moral motivation in the political leadership that political leaders must be able to justify their decisions on moral grounds. They may not act primarily or solely for the right, but they must have some reason, producible on request, for thinking that they are acting for the right, among other things. For those who let slip the dogs of war, it is not sufficient that things turn out for the best. The evils of even a just war are sufficiently great that we can demand of leaders who initiate war that they understand the moral character of the results they seek.

If desire for the right must be included as one of the motives for just war, are there any motives that must be *excluded*? Various authors have insisted that a just war cannot be motivated by love of violence or hatred of the enemy. Even in the fifth century Augustine wrote, "The real evils in war are love of violence, vengeful cruelty, fierce and implacable enmity, wild resistance, lust for power, and the like" (*Contra Faustum*, XXII.75). Most people will agree that a leader who has love of violence or hatred of the enemy as his sole or chief motivation for war has a bad intention. But Augustine and other authors go further and argue that it is immoral to make war if hatred is just one of the many motivations one has for fighting. The rule is severe, but worth considering.

Consider the American campaign against Japan in World War II. By the usual standards, the American decision to fight against Japan satisfied the rules of just war. But as the war proceeded, many Americans, stirred up by wartime propaganda, were seized with racial animosity and came to hate all Japanese as such. The 4-year internment of 180,000 innocent Japanese Americans, the campaign of extermination against Japanese cities, and the attack on Hiroshima were all caused or rendered tolerable by this atmosphere of hate. Observing this, Augustine would condemn this hatred of the Japanese as sin and the war against Japan as unjust. Nevertheless, it would be unreasonable to tell the relatives of those who died at Pearl Harbor or on Bataan that they should not feel hatred toward those whose acts and decisions took the lives of those they loved.

The difficulties concerning hatred can perhaps be resolved by distinguishing justifiable from unjustifiable hatred. Hatred of leaders who choose to wage unjust war is justifiable; hatred of their compatriots and coracialists is not, since hatred of human beings as such—apart from their voluntary acts—is not a morally acceptable emotion. By this standard, American leaders who chose wartime policies as a result of race hatred toward the Japanese were not engaged in just war, even if their policies were acceptable by all other moral tests.

4. JUST CAUSE

The most important of the *jus ad bellum* rules is the rule that the moral use of military force requires a just cause. From the earliest writings, just war theorists rejected love of war and love of conquest as morally acceptable causes for war: "We [should] wage war," Aristotle wrote, "for the sake of peace" (*Politics*, 1333A) Likewise, the seizure of plunder was always rejected as an acceptable cause for war. Beyond these elementary restrictions, however, a wide variety of "just causes" were recognized. The history of the subject is the history of how this repertoire of just causes was progressively cut down to the modern standard, which accepts only the single cause of self-defense.

As early as Cicero in the first century B.C., analysts of just war recognized that the only proper occasion for the use of force was a "wrong received." It follows from this that the condition or characteristics of potential enemies, apart from their actions, cannot supply a just cause for war. Aristotle's suggestion that a war is justified to enslave those who naturally deserve to be slaves, John Stuart Mill's claim that military intervention is justified in order to bestow the benefits of Western civilization on less advanced peoples, and the historically common view that forcible conversion to some true faith is justified as obedience to divine command are all invalidated by the absence of a "wrong received."

Obviously, the concept of a "wrong received" stands in need of considerable analysis. In the eighteenth century, the notion of wrong included the notion of insult, and sovereigns considered it legitimate to initiate war in response to verbal disrespect, desecrations of national symbols, and so forth. The nineteenth century, which saw the abolition of private duels, likewise saw national honor reduced to a secondary role in the moral justification of war. For most nineteenth century theorists, the primary wrongs were not insults, but acts or policies of a government resulting in violations of the rights of the nation waging just war.

By twentieth-century standards, this definition of international wrongs providing conditions of just war was both too restrictive and too loose. It was too restrictive in that it failed to recognize any rights of *peoples*, as opposed to *states*: rights to cultural integrity, national self-determination, and so forth. It was too loose in that it sanctioned the use of military force in response to wrongs the commission of which may not have involved military force, thus condoning, on occasion, the first use of arms.

These two excesses were abolished in twentieth-century international law. The right to national self-determination was a prevailing theme at the Versailles conference in 1919 and was repeatedly invoked in the period of decolonization following World War II. Prohibition of first use of force was attempted in drafting of the U. N. Charter in 1945:

> Article 2(4): All Members shall refrain in their international relations from the threat or use of force against the territorial integrity or political independence of any state or in any other manner inconsistent with the Purposes of the United Nations.
> Article 51: Nothing in the present Charter shall impair the inherent right of individual or collective self-defense if an armed attack occurs against a member of the United Nations, until the Security Council has taken the measures necessary to maintain international peace and security.

Strictly speaking, Article 51 does not prohibit first use of military force: to say that explicitly, the phrase "if an armed attack occurs" would have to be replaced by "if and only if an armed attack occurs." Nevertheless, Article 51, coupled with article 2(4), rules out anticipatory self-defense. Legitimate self-defense must be self-defense against an actual attack.

The U. N. Charter represents the most restrictive analysis of just cause in the history of the subject. In discussions since, members of the United Nations have continued to assume that just cause consists only in self-defense, but "self-defense" has come to be understood as a response to aggression. The definition of "aggression" thus becomes central to the analysis of just cause. In the United Nations, a special committee established to analyze the concept of aggression produced a definition adopted by the General Assembly on 14 December 1974:

> *Article 1.* Aggression is the use of armed force by a State against the sovereignty, territorial integrity, or political independence of another State, or in any other manner inconsistent with the Charter of the United Nations. . . .
> *Article 2.* The first use of armed force by a State in contravention the Charter shall constitute *prima facie* evidence of an act of aggression [although the Security Council may come to determine that an act of aggression has not in fact been committed]. . . .

Article 3. Any of the following acts regardless of a declaration of war shall . . . qualify as an act of aggression:

(a) The invasion or attack by the armed force of a State on the territory of another State, or any military occupation, however temporary;

(b) Bombardment by the armed forces of a State against the territory of another State;

(c) The blockade of the ports or coasts of a State by the armed forces of another State;

(d) An attack by the armed forces of a State on the land, sea, air, or marine and air fleets of another State; . . .

(g) The sending by or on behalf of a State of armed bands, groups, irregulars, or mercenaries, which carry out acts of armed force against another State of such gravity as to amount to the acts listed above. . . .

Article 4. The acts enumerated are not exhaustive.

Article 5. No consideration of whatever nature, whether political, economic, military, or otherwise, may serve as a justification for aggression. . . .

Article 7. Nothing in this definition . . . could in any way prejudice the right to self-determination, freedom, and independence, as derived from the Charter, of peoples forcibly deprived of that right . . . particularly peoples under colonial and racist regimes or other forms of alien domination; nor the right of these peoples to struggle to that end and to seek and receive support. . . .

By reading between the lines, the intent of the special committee can be easily discerned. In failing to enumerate under "acts of aggression" such traditional causes of war as attacks on citizens abroad, assaults on nonmilitary ships and aircraft on the high seas, and the seizure of property of aliens, the committee counted as aggression only military acts that might substantially affect the physical security of the nation suffering aggression. The only violation of rights that merits the unilateral use of force by nations is the physically threatening use of force by another state.

5. ANTICIPATION AND JUST CAUSE

One of the most radical features of the United Nations analysis of just cause is its rejection of anticipatory self-defense. The decision of those who framed the Charter was informed by history: the argument of anticipatory self-defense had been repeatedly and cynically invoked by political leaders set on military adventures, and the framers were determined to prevent a repetition of August 1914, when nations declared war in response to mobilizations, that is, to anticipated attacks rather than actual attacks. The U. N. view stands on good logical ground: if the use of force by nation A is justified on the grounds that its rights have been violated by Nation B, then nation B must have already done something that has violated A's rights. To argue that force is necessary in order to *prevent* a future rights violation by nation B is not to make an argument based on rights at all: it is a call to use force in order to make a better world—a very different sort of moral argument than the argument that a right has been violated, and one rejected by the mainstream tradition that defines just war as a response to a "wrong received."

Nevertheless, many scholars are uncomfortable with an absolute ban on anticipatory self-defense. It might be wise, as a point of international law, to reject anticipatory self-defense in order to deprive nations of a convenient legal pretext for war, but from the point of view of moral principles, it is implausible that *every* case of anticipatory self-defense should be morally wicked. After all, people accept the morality of ordinary self-defense on the grounds that cases arise in which survival requires force directed against the attacker, and the use of force is morally proper in such cases. But exactly the same argument, "the use of force when necessary for survival," could be made in some cases of anticipatory self-defense.

Israel and the Six-Day War

The most frequently discussed example in the study of anticipatory self-defense is the Israeli attack on Egypt on 5 June 1967.

In the spring of 1967, tension mounted between Israel and Syria in the wake of a Syrian coup that brought the socialist Ba'ath regime to power. On 16 May, Syria mobilized its forces, and simultaneously in Egypt, President Nasser ordered U. N. peacekeeping forces to leave the Sinai, where they had been stationed since 1956, in part to guarantee free access through the Straits of Tiran, Israel's only access to the Red Sea. In response to the withdrawal of U. N. troops, Israel mobilized, and Egypt followed suit. On 23 May, Nasser blockaded the Straits of Tiran, sealing off the Israeli Red Sea port of Eilat. Should this action lead to war, Nasser announced, the result would be the destruction of Israel. On 1 June, Jordan entered into military alliance with Egypt, and an Iraqi division entered Jordan. On 5 June, at 8:15 A.M., the Israeli Air Force attacked and destroyed 300 of Egypt's 340 service-ready combat aircraft. Six days later, the war ended with the complete defeat of all Arab forces and a 400 percent increase in the size of the State of Israel.

Since Israel was the first to attack, supporters of Israel commonly describe the actions of 5 June as anticipatory self-defense, arguing that it was reasonable to believe that an Arab attack was forthcoming. Furthermore, authors like Michael Walzer argue that the blockade of the Straits of Tiran, and the strain of an ongoing mobilization, constituted a military threat of sufficient magnitude as to imperil Israel's existence, morally justifying a first use of force. But perhaps it is not necessary to describe Israeli actions in 1967 as anticipatory self-defense at all. If self-defense is the use of force in response to aggression, then the Israeli attack can be viewed as self-defense in response to aggression constituted by the Egyptian blockade of the Straits of Tiran. Blockades have traditionally been considered acts of war, and blockades were prominently listed as acts of aggression in the 1977 U. N. definition of aggression quoted above. By this standard, Israeli actions are simple self-defense, not anticipatory self-defense.

6. INTERVENTION AND JUST CAUSE

At first sight it would appear that the U. N. Charter rules out the use of force by all nations except the victims of aggression. But there is an escape clause in Article 51, which grants nations the right of *collective* self-defense. In cases of legitimate collective self-defense, a nation can permissibly use force against an aggressor without itself being the victim of aggression.

So far as international law and custom are concerned, most scholars are agreed that legitimate use of force by A on behalf of B against aggressor C requires some prior mutual defense agreement between A and B. The legal logic of this interpretation of collective self-defense is straightforward: the main intent of the U. N. Charter is to prevent nations from having recourse to force, and to achieve this end it would not be a good idea to let any nation rush to the aid of any other nation that seems to be the victim of aggression. But international law here may be too strict for our moral sensibilities. We do not, at the personal level, require the Good Samaritans have prior contracts with those they seek to aid, even if the Good Samaritan, unlike his biblical predecessor, must use force to rescue the victim of attack. By analogy it seems unreasonable to require prior collective defense agreements between international Good Samaritans and nations that are the victims of aggression.

The cases of collective self-defense that have standing in international law are cases in which one nation intervenes in a quarrel between two other states. But there are many cases in which governments are tempted to intervene in a conflict *within* another state, a conflict between subnational groups or between subnational groups and national government. Defining just cause for interventions in these internal disputes is far more difficult. A long tradition of international law treats most such interventions as reprehensible violations of national sovereignty. The justification of self-defense is patently inapplicable. In history, the majority of such interventions have had immoral motives, disastrous results, or both. Yet every author who writes about this subject has a list of favorite cases in which, it is felt, military intervention was morally justified, or would have been.

The main argument against these interventions is that they violate the right of national sovereignty, recognized in international law. But though recognition in international law establishes a *legal* right, it cannot establish a *moral* right, since the law might itself be immoral. Should national sovereignty be accepted as a *moral* right? Does it make sense to attribute moral rights to *nations* as such?

Some believe that only individual persons can have moral rights. The possession of moral rights is logically connected to the possession of moral responsibilities, and moral responsibilities can be assigned only to entities capable of free choices. But only individual persons are capable of free choices; nations, which are aggregates of persons, do not possess consciousness, and "make choices" only in a metaphorical sense. Furthermore, a moral right is a moral warrant to make demands and undertake actions that are contrary to majority preference and to the common good. Moral theories that take rights seriously postulate such rights for persons on the grounds that individuals have the right to undertake projects and careers at some cost to the general interest, since self-chosen lives are the highest repositories of value in human life. No such rationales could be extended to the choices of nations, first, because they do not make choices, and second, because it seems intolerable that a nation should be morally justified in pursuing interests detrimental to the welfare of the world. To speak of "the rights of nations" is like speaking about "the average American family," something that doesn't really exist, though rights exist and families exist.

If only individual persons have rights, then the so-called rights of *nations* are derived from the rights of individual persons, and governments and political leaders pursuing policies in the name of the "nation" are morally justified only to the degree that their policies fulfill or defend the rights of their constituents: the only right of a state is the right to defend the rights of its citizens. If the government and the political leaders pursue policies that suppress the rights of their own people, then they cannot defend those policies against principled, Good Samaritan interventions on grounds of a right of national sovereignty.

Intervention, then, in the face of rights violation by a government may have just cause. But *which* rights violations provide just cause for interventions? It would be a grave mistake to sanction intervention in face of rights violations of every type. It would not be appropriate for nation A to intervene in nation B because nation B has closed down its free press, nor would it be appropriate for nation C to intervene in D if D permits private ownership of the means of production and expropriation of surplus value from the working class, even if we believe in rights to free expression and freedom from exploitation. Such a proliferation of just causes for intervention would lead to endless war. Rather, it is reasonable to limit violations of national sovereignty to cases in which a government has violated the basic values national sovereignty is supposed to protect: the physical safety of the citizens and their freedom from alien domination. Furthermore, the intervention must be requested, or at least welcomed, by the persons whose rights it is supposed to protect. Otherwise, one must assume that the rights in question have been waived, and the justification for intervention disappears.

(a)   The Indo-Pakistani War of 1971

One case that meets these standards—a frequently cited example of justified intervention—is the Indian intervention in East Pakistan in 1971. In December 1970, the Awami League, a movement for greater regional autonomy in Bengali East Pakistan, won a majority in the National Assembly of Pakistan, a nation consisting of two separate territories to the east and west of India. Bending to opposition in West Pakistan, General Yahya Khan indefinitely postponed the opening of the National Assembly, an act that led to widespread agitation in East Pakistan. Khan responded by sending in the Pakistani Army, staffed by non-Bengalis. The Army began arresting Awami League members and soon shifted to a policy of wholesale slaughter of Bengali leaders, down to the village level. The numbers of dead were in the hundreds of thousands, and an ensuing famine may have killed millions. By November, over 6 million Bengali refugees had fled for food and safety into India. On 4 December the Indian Army smashed into East Bengal; on 16 December, Dacca was liberated. Pakistani forces surrendered, Indian forces withdrew, and the nation of Bangladesh was born. Protests from Rawalpindi that the Indian attack violated Pakistani sovereignty were absurd: in East Pakistan, the Rawalpindi government was engaged in rights violations on a massive scale; it had no moral sovereignty that it could lose.

(b)   The Osirak Raid of 1981

Few interventions are so morally clear-cut as India's in 1971. Consider a more problematic case: the raid into Iraq by Israeli fighter bombers that destroyed the nuclear reactor under construction at Osirak in 1981. The Osirak reactor was capable of producing weapons-grade plutonium, and the Israelis could not be blamed if they rejected the argument that Iraq—an oil-rich nation—needed nuclear reactors to generate electricity. The possession of nuclear bombs by the Iraqis would constitute a grave threat to the security of Israel and the safety of the whole world, and the Israeli raid was neatly confined to the elimination of this threat. At the same time, the construction of the Osirak reactor violated no rights of Iraqi citizens, and the Israelis could scarcely claim that Iraqi citizens had invited them to make the attack. The raid did more good then harm but, in the absence of rights violations by the Iraqis, it lacked just cause.

7.   THE RULE OF PROPORTIONALITY

It is a superficially paradoxical feature of just war theory that a just cause need not make for a just war. If the just cause can be achieved by some means other than war, then war for that just cause is not morally justified. If the just cause *might* be achieved by other means that have not been attempted, then war for that just cause is not just war. If the cause is just but cannot be achieved by war, then war for that cause is not just war. These rules, sometimes called the rule of necessity, the rule of last resort, or the "chance of victory" requirement, are part of that section of just war theory which acknowledges that some just causes are not sufficiently weighty, on the moral scales, to justify the evils that war for those just causes might produce. The rule of proportionality states that a war cannot be just unless the evil that can reasonably be expected to ensue from the war is less than the evil that can reasonably be expected to ensue if the war is not fought.

The rule of proportionality is easy to state but hard to interpret, since there are no guidelines as to what counts as an "evil" when the rule is applied. Suppose that we interpret an "evil" as a loss of value, that is, as death, injury, physical and psychological suffering, misery, and so forth. On this view of evil, the rule of proportionality implies that a war is just only if there will be more death, suffering, and so forth if the war is not fought than if the war is fought: a just and proportionate war does more good than harm. Given the destructiveness of war, the rule of proportionality, on this interpretation, would declare that almost all wars, even wars with just causes, have been unjust wars.

Suppose that we count as "evils" not merely losses of welfare but also losses that are violations of someone's rights. Then the rule of proportionality implies that a war is just if more rights would be violated if the war is not fought than if the war is fought. Since we have defined a just cause as a cause that seeks to prevent violations of rights, on this interpretation of the rule of proportionality, almost all wars with just causes have been proportionate wars.

Which interpretation of "evil" is the most appropriate for the moral analysis of war? If we interpret "evil" as "violation of rights," then the rule of proportionality, which was supposed to provide an additional and independent check on the moral permissibility of war, is subsumed into the requirement of just cause. If the rule of proportionality is to do any work, we must consider an "evil" to be the destruction of a value. But then the problem arises that the rule condemns almost all wars and reduces just war theory to antiwar pacifism. Some revision of the rule is in order.

From the standpoint of theories of moral rights, a rule which says that war is unjust unless it does more good than harm is far too restrictive. If a war has a just cause, then it is a war in defense of rights and, according to most theories of rights, the maintenance and protection of rights is morally permissible unless the defense of rights causes *a great deal* more harm than good. Accordingly, in just war theory, we can replace the traditional principle—a just war must cause more good than harm—with the less restrictive rule that a war for a just cause passes the test of proportionality unless it produces a *great deal* more harm than good. Even this greatly liberalized rule of proportionality will declare that many wars fought for just causes have been unjust wars, since many wars for just causes have in fact produced a great deal more harm than good. On the other hand, if a war is fought for a just cause and produces only slightly more harm than good, the liberalized rule of proportionality will not judge that war to be unjust.

8.   WEIGHING JUST CAUSE AGAINST PROPORTIONALITY

All just causes are just, but some are more just than others. The amount of harm that it is morally permissible to produce in pursuit of a just cause should be a function of the moral importance of the cause. No formula can be generated for weighing the justice of the cause against the harm that might be done in pursuing it; the question can be resolved only on a case-by-case basis, by persons with a grasp of the relevant facts and sufficient strength of character to view the problem from an impersonal rather than a patriotic point of view.

(a) Belgium 1914

Consider the position of the Belgians as World War I began. On 2 August 1914, a German minister to Belgium handed King Albert an ultimatum demanding free passage for German armies proceeding from Germany through Belgium to France. The king promptly refused, and Belgium prepared to resist scores of German divisions with just six of its own. Though Belgian resistance was gallant and surprisingly stiff at Liège, the German armies were delayed just two days by Belgian military opposition, and the losses to Belgium were immense. Though the Belgian cause was just, considerations of proportionality indicate that a decision not to fight would not have been immoral.

(b) Finland 1939

Considerations of proportionality weigh even more heavily against the decision of the Finns to resist the Russians in 1939. Despite the Hitler-Stalin pact, Stalin was sufficiently suspicious of the Nazis to seek a defensible western border, and this required that the Russian border be moved north, away from Leningrad. (Events in the subsequent siege of Leningrad proved this assessment to be essentially correct.) Stalin asked the Finns to sell territory that would realign the border, and the Finns refused. On 30 November 1939, the Russians attacked. Though the Finns, under Baron von Mannerheim, fought brilliantly through the winter, they collapsed before numerically superior forces in March 1940. As with Belgium in 1914, the Finnish cause was just. At the same time, Stalin's aims were manifestly limited, and the justice of the Finnish cause, one might argue, did not outweigh the destruction that could be expected from resistance. If so, the Finnish decision to resist was disproportionately harmful, and both sides fought an unjust war.

(c) The Six-Day War Revisited

Because of the blockade of the Straits of Tiran, the Israelis could claim that their attack on Egypt was undertaken in self-defense. Thus, the Israelis had just cause. The question is still open, however, whether the Six-Day War was necessary and proportionate. First, if the Israelis had not attacked, war might have been avoided and 20,000 lives saved. (This argument cannot be rebutted on the grounds that we cannot know what might have happened if Israel had not attacked, since the Israeli case is equally based on assumptions about what might have happened if they had not attacked.) Second, the blockade of the Straits of Tiran, though serious, was not life-threatening to Israel, since there were open and unblockadable Israeli ports on the Mediterranean. Third, the strain of mobilization was at least as costly to Egypt as to Israel, and Arab troops would soon have had to stand down. Fourth, if the Israelis had not preempted and the Arabs had attacked first, the State of Israel would nevertheless have survived, since this was precisely what happened when greatly augmented Arab forces struck first in 1973.

In applying the rule of proportionality to the Six-Day War, we must consider not only the destruction that the war did cause, but also the destruction that the Israelis might have expected the war to cause before they began it. On 5 June 1967, the Israelis had no strong evidence that they were about to win one of the most astounding military victories in modern warfare, and that the war would be over in just six days. They had reason to expect that the war would be much longer and bloodier than it was, and it is all these *expected* deaths that must be weighed against the middling importance of reopening the Straits of Tiran.

(d) Extreme Emergency

There is one type of the justice-versus-proportionality problem that especially interests the just war theorist: cases in which the just cause is the continued existence of the state itself. Some might argue that any amount of force, causing any amount of harm, is morally justified if necessary for national survival. Is this reasonable?

Suppose that the state threatened with annihilation (call it state X) has started an unjust war that it is now on the verge of losing to enemies that have called for unconditional surrender, or that state X is the subject of morally justifiable intervention or morally justifiable revolution. In such cases, since state X has been a perpetrator of injustice, it would be bizarre to say that its continued existence is of such moral importance that it has the right to inflict great harm in order to preserve itself.

Now suppose that state X is innocent but cannot save itself except by actions that produce immense quantities of death and suffering. Can these quantities ever be so great that state X loses its right to self-defense? On the personal level, the right to self-defense entitles an innocent person to take actions that cause considerable destruction. If an innocent person is attacked by 20 people and has no recourse, he is entitled to kill all 20 if he can. By analogy, it would seem that one innocent nation is morally entitled to destroy 20 aggressor states if it can and if such an act is necessary for its survival. But the analogy is a poor one, since in the personal case, all 20 attackers are guilty, whereas, when a nation makes war, even just war, many innocent people are killed. The proper question to raise at the personal level is this: How many innocent people am I entitled to kill if their deaths are necessary for my own survival? Even for nonpacifists, the answer is "not many." It follows, at the level of nations, that the right of a state to cause destruction in order to assure its own survival is not unlimited.

9. THE RULE OF JUST PEACE

The preceding sections considered all the traditional rules of *jus ad bellum*. Since the rules are addressed to decision makers contemplating war, they take into consideration only such facts as are available to decision makers before war begins. There is room for one further rule, a rule that takes into consideration facts available to moral judges after the war ends. For war to be just, the winning side must not only have obtained justice for itself; it must not have achieved it at the price of violating the rights of others. A just war must lead to a just peace.

The rule of just outcome provides a solution to an ancient controversy concerning just cause. In the modern analysis, for nation A to have just cause, its rights must have been violated by nation B. Pursuit of this just cause permits nation A to use force to restore its rights. But do the rules of morality restrict A to just the restoration of its rights? In civil law, if party B has wrongfully injured party A, A is often entitled not just to compensation for the loss sustained through the injury but also to damages. By analogy, a nation acting in self-defense is entitled not merely to a restoration of the status quo ante but also to further rewards. In considering the scope of these rewards, authors have looked charitably on such rewards as might provide nation A with improved security in the future and teach the lesson that international crime does not pay.

The analogy, however, between civil law and international affairs is weak. The party that pays damages in civil law deserves to be forced to pay, but changes in international arrangements resulting from successful wars fought in self-defense may involve thousands of persons who were not parties to the conflict. It is in the interest of these victims of international upheaval that the rule of just outcome be applied. Such acts as go beyond the restoration of the status quo ante, acts that provide the victor with improved security or assess damages against the loser, must not violate the rights of the citizens in the losing nation or the rights of third parties.

(a) Korea 1950

A common textbook example of the use of force beyond the permissible limits of self-defense is Gen. Douglas MacArthur's thrust to the Yalu River in Korea in 1950.

In June 1950, troops from North Korea pushed into South Korea, nearly overrunning the country and bringing down the South Korean government in Seoul. After the successful landing at Inchon in September, MacArthur's troops reached and crossed the North Korean border in October, then moved north to the Chinese border at the Yalu River. The Chinese counterattacked en masse in November, driving American (and U. N.) forces far to the south. After three more years of fighting, the best that could be said for American efforts was reestablishment of a putative national division between North and South Korea, back at the original border.

If the United States had simply sought a restoration of that status quo ante, MacArthur should have stopped at the North Korean border in October 1950. Nevertheless, given the injustice of North Korea's attack and its manifest desire to impose its rule over the much larger population of South Korea, it *was* morally permissible to continue military operations northward; replacement of the North Korean government would not have been a manifestly unjust outcome. MacArthur's problem was not so much a breach of the principle of just peace as an imprudent estimation of the Chinese reaction to military forces marching in their direction.

(b) 1967 Yet Again

A more interesting test of the rule of just outcome is the long-term results of the Six-Day War. Let us assume that our previous analysis was correct and that the Israelis were acting in self-defense against Egyptian aggression, and let us assume, contrary to the previous discussion, that Israeli actions satisfied the rule of proportionality. Israel, then, was morally justified in using force to reopen the Straits of Tiran. Since the straits could not be reopened without war with Egypt *and* Jordan *and* Syria, the Israelis, on these assumptions, were morally justified in attacking all three nations. A restoration of the status quo ante would consist of reopening of the straits, together with military and diplomatic guarantees that they would remain open. By the sixth day of war, the Israelis had not merely reopened the straits but also had established military dominion over the Sinai, the Gaza Strip, the West Bank, East Jerusalem, and the Golan Heights, all of which, save for the Sinai, they control to this day.

In these territories live over 900,000 Arabs who have no prospect of Israeli citizenship and no desire to live at the dictates of the Israeli government. Of the occupied territories, only the retention of the Golan Heights can be justified on grounds of military necessity. (The Israeli government sometimes argues for the retention of the West Bank not on military reasons but on the grounds that "Judea and Samaria" were parts of biblical Israel.) If the blockade of the Straits of Tiran was aggression, the Six-Day War began justly. But by depriving nearly a million people of governments they preferred to Israel's, it did not end justly. By the principle of just peace, the Six-Day War was not a just war.

10. JUS AD BELLUM AND VIETNAM

No war and no act of intervention stirred more controversy in the United States than the Vietnam War. We will take up the decision to intervene in Vietnam rule by rule. The United States was seriously involved in the Vietnam conflict from 1950 on, supporting the French in a losing struggle to keep Indochina a colony of France. But for the United States, the point at which to apply the rules of just war is 8 March 1965, when U. S. Marines waded ashore at Danang. Ten years later the war ended, and 57,000 Americans and a million Vietnamese were dead.

(a) Competent Authority?

The war in which the United States intervened was a war between the government in Saigon and the National Liberation Front (NLF). In nominal control of all of Vietnam south of the seventeenth parallel, the Saigon regime had been established in October 1955, when Ngo Dinh Diem declared himself president of the Republic of Vietnam. Diem had been assassinated in 1963, but his successors—Duong Van Minh, Nguyen Khanh, Phan Huy Quat, and, finally, Nguyen Cao Ky and Nguyen Van Thieu—continued Diem's opposition to the unification of North Vietnam and South Vietnam—called for in international agreements signed in 1955—and to social revolution or reform in the South. The NLF, in 1965, was a coalition of South Vietnamese Buddhists, social reformers, socialists, and Communists, committed primarily to social change in South Vietnam but also interested in the reunification of Vietnam, acting with some degree of support from the Communist regime of Ho Chi Minh in the North.

Did the Saigon regime have "competent authority," that is, sufficient competence to wage a just war and to invite foreigners to use force inside South Vietnam? According to some authors, the Saigon regime was competent because (a) it functioned like a competent government—collected taxes, built roads, maintained bridges, delivered the mail, and so forth; (b) because it exercised control over identifiable territory, including the capital; and (c) because it exercised control "by responsible command" over its military forces.

Dissenting scholars argue that the Saigon regime was not competent (a) because it was established contrary to an international agreement that had brought peace to Vietnam in 1955, an agreement that called for free elections in 1956 which Diem had *prevented* from taking place; (b) because the majority of people throughout Vietnam considered Vietnam a single nation, which the Saigon regime had artificially divided; and, most of all, (c) because no government in Saigon could have held power for six months were it not for massive and continuous infusions of American aid. Opponents of the war believed that it was ridiculous to argue that American intervention was justified because the Saigon government "asked" for help, when the Saigon government was, in some sense, paid to ask us in, should it find itself unable to hold back the revolutionary tide.

The argument that the Saigon regime was an American puppet and not a legitimate national government deserves careful analysis. Let us assume that Diem and his successors could not have stood for very long on their own. For many, this suffices to show that the Saigon government lacked authority and, therefore, the right to use military force. But supporters of Saigon in 1965 might argue that the fact that a government needs help to subsist does not prove that it is illegitimate. The American Revolution, for example, could not have been won without help from the French, but nobody argues today that the Washington's use of force was immoral because colonies he defended could not stand on their own. The phrase "stand on their own" is troublesome and ambiguous. One could say of any government in the world that in the absence of certain supporting conditions, the government would collapse. For South Vietnam, the supporting condition was American aid. But the government did function, and for many years substantial numbers of South Vietnamese were prepared to die in its defense.

Opponents of American intervention will rush to point out that the analogy between George Washington and Diem is weak. The American revolutionaries declared independence without French prompting; they held on for several years with little French aid; they determined policy apart from French wishes; they developed a constitution and submitted it for ratification; and Washington stood in a general election before becoming president. Diem was brought in and propped up by the United States to carry out foreign wishes; he never submitted a constitution and hardly felt constrained by such laws as there were; and he never stood for election, because all sides knew that in a vote Ho Chi Minh would certainly carry all of Vietnam and probably even the South by itself. For all these reasons, Diem and his successors could be considered agents of the Americans. If so, American intervention fails to qualify as one nation assisting in the self-defense of another.

Defenders of American intervention complained bitterly through the Vietnam years that critics of the war used different standards when judging American conduct and the conduct of the NLF. So we must ask: Was the NLF a competent revolutionary movement? Did it have the moral authority to use force?

Certainly the NLF in 1965 had military forces under responsible command, and had large sections of the countryside under control by day and even larger sections under control by night: in 41 of 44 South Vietnamese provinces, the NLF was regularly collecting taxes. These are the usual legal criteria for belligerent status. But if we dismiss the competence of the Saigon regime for its inability to subsist without American aid, should we not dismiss the competence of the NLF for its inability to subsist without support from North Vietnam?

Two arguments suggest that the NFL case is different. First of all, from the time of its founding in 1960 through 1965, the NLF appears to have received very little material support from North Vietnam; certainly it received from Hanoi but a small fraction of the support that Saigon received from Washington. (North Vietnam became increasingly involved after 1965, but an intervention in 1965 must be judged by the conditions of 1965.) Second, support from Hanoi was support for Vietnamese people by Vietnamese people. Such aid could be seen as part of an effort for national self-determination, which is a right of peoples recognized by the community of nations. From the first, the Americans assumed that they were fighting Communism, but more than anything they were fighting Vietnamese nationalism, which was as strong in the South as it was in the North. Had they been fighting only Communism, they might have won.

(b) Right Intention?

The United States had many intentions in Vietnam, so many that it is difficult to locate a dominant intention. The most frequently announced intention was that the United States was fighting so that the South Vietnamese people could freely determine what government they wanted. This explanation was difficult to sustain in light of the fact that Diem, with American support, had scuttled the general elections of 1956, and that no subsequent South Vietnamese leader could match the prestige and popularity of Ho Chi Minh. If there was a dominant American hope, it was to prevent the establishment of a Communist government in South Vietnam—*regardless* of South Vietnamese attitudes—a hope motivated by the idea that Communism would be a bad thing for South Vietnam and by the idea that a victory over Communism would be a good thing for American credibility in its global cold war.

If the dominant American intention was prevention of an outcome deemed harmful to the Vietnamese, then American intentions, traditionally rated, were altruistic and morally acceptable. If the dominant American intention was to strike a blow against world Communism that would improve American prestige and world standing, then the United States was using Vietnam as a pawn and American intentions were not morally acceptable. Which intention dominated the American decision to intervene? Did American policy makers really care what happened to the Vietnamese people? Did they really have their interests at heart? Were they prepared to sacrifice American prestige if the interests of the Vietnamese people demanded it? Did their interactions with the Vietnamese from the Saigon government down through the peasants express respect for people regarded as moral equals?

Many people familiar with events in Vietnam through 1965, people who know how the United States trained Diem's secret police and how they behaved, how at American instigation tens of thousands of peasants were uprooted from traditional villages and thrown into armed encampments, how American responses and judgments were biased by the racist attitudes that continued to infect American relations with Asian peoples, believe that the American leadership thought first about world politics and only second about the Vietnamese. In affirming the American commitment to Diem, a mandarin Catholic dictator in a land of Buddhist peasants, President Kennedy revealed his intentions to James Reston in 1961: "We have a problem making our power credible, and Vietnam looks like the place" (Stanley Karnow, *Vietnam: A History*, p. 248).

(c) Just Cause?

Much of the analysis of just cause in the case of Vietnam is tied to considerations of competent authority. But let us assume that the Saigon regime was competent and had the authority to use force. Did it have just cause to use it? In the modern analysis, just cause is restricted to self-defense, and in assessing the claims of self-defense, it is crucial to consider who used force first and where it was used.

When Vietnam was divided in 1955, there were many people in South Vietnam who had supported or participated in the Vietminh, Ho Chi Minh's movement against the French colonial regime. In 1955 and 1956, thousands of Vietminh cadres and leftist sympathizers in the South were subjected to arrest, torture, prison, and execution by the Diem government. At the same time, Ho Chi Minh had been persuaded to desist from military operations in the South in hopes of winning a political victory in the elections of 1956, elections that Diem refused to hold. In these years, then, what we have in Vietnam is a police action—indistinguishable in a dictatorship from military operations—against a political movement. Since the NLF did not begin its campaign of violence on any scale before 1961, the first use of force *in the South* was by the regime in Saigon.

Defenders of American intervention generally view the Vietnam conflict not as an internal struggle *in* South Vietnam but as a war *between* the states of North and South Vietnam. Do the actions of North Vietnam in these years constitute a use of force such that Saigon and Washington could claim that their actions against North Vietnam were acts of self-defense?

No one denies that North Vietnam aided the NLF from 1960 through 1965. But if one runs through the list of acts of aggression formulated by the U. N. special committee on the definition of aggression, none of the acts described there fit the acts of North Vietnam, and the level of North Vietnamese support, as we noted, was a small fraction of the support Washington provided to the Saigon regime. The U. S. State Department, which had every reason to exaggerate, claimed in 1965 that 40,000 North Vietnamese troops had entered South Vietnam since 1955, but that figure amounts to only 4,000 per year. The State Department did not claim that these troops mounted military operations against South Vietnamese forces, nor did it explain how it distinguished North Vietnamese from NLF cadres.

South Vietnamese naval commandos under American direction began taking the fight to North Vietnamese territory in the summer of 1964. After a South Vietnamese raid on 30 July against several North Vietnamese islands, North Vietnamese PT boats engaged the U. S. Destroyer *Maddox*, which was patrolling the Tonkin Gulf in the general area of these raids. On 4 August, PT boats approached and may or may not have shot at the *Maddox* and the U.S.S. *Turner Joy*, which may or may not have been in the North Vietnamese territorial waters—the accounts are contradictory. At any rate, no damage was done. President Johnson responded on 5 August by ordering an air raid that destroyed most of North Vietnam's small navy and a significant fraction of its oil-refining capacity.

Given subsequent events, historians will debate forever about North Vietnam's infiltration and the Tonkin Gulf incidents. But it is clear that by March 1965 the South Vietnamese and their American allies had used considerably more direct force against North Vietnam than North Vietnam had directed against the South.

(d) Proportionality?

In our treatment of proportionality, we noted that the amount of harm justifiable in military action should be proportionate to the justice of the cause. The justice of American intervention in Vietnam, however, is hotly debated; and if the justice of the cause is debatable, then the proportionality of the means used to achieve it will be debatable as well. To make the discussion of proportionality more interesting, let us assume that the real issue in the war was not the social reforms sought by the NLF but the unification of the country under rule from Hanoi, and let us assume that the prevention of reunification was a just cause: that rule from Hanoi would violate the rights of people in South Vietnam in some fundamentally different and more malevolent way than their rights were violated under the Saigon regime. After these concessions to the defender of intervention, the question of proportionality is this: Was the harm to be expected from the effort to achieve this cause substantially greater than the evil that would be produced if the cause of South Vietnam was abandoned?

Most people in the United States today feel that the Vietnam War "wasn't worth the effort." For many hawks and doves alike, the harms done to American soldiers and the overall costs of the war do not seem proportionate to the importance of the cause. But this popular judgment is prompted by the knowledge that the war was lost, and that knowledge was not available to policy makers in 1965. Given the information available in 1965, and given the harm that could be reasonably expected to ensue from American intervention, did the intervention meet the test of proportionality?

Defenders of intervention believe that it did. Professor William O'Brien argues, for example, that the harm to be expected from intervention in Vietnam could best be estimated by extrapolation from American experience in Korea. Since, in O'Brien's view, the harm done in Korea was justified by the justice of keeping South Korea free from North Korea's Kim Il Sung, the harm to be expected in Vietnam was justified by the justice of keeping South Vietnam free from Ho Chi Minh.

Opponents of intervention will protest that there was plenty of evidence available in 1965 to show that the success in Vietnam would not come as easily as success in Korea, and that the damage done in Vietnam by American intervention would dwarf the damage done to Korea, great as it was. First, the population of South Korea was more than double North Korea's; the populations of North and South Vietnam were roughly equal. Second, the North Koreans attempted to conquer South Korea by brute force; they had little support in the South and no apparatus for political control. The NLF had developed an elaborate political mechanism in South Vietnam and had the support of a substantial fraction of the population. Third, the leader in South Korea, Syngman Rhee, had credentials in the struggle against foreign control (in this case, the Japanese) at least as credible as Kim Il Sung's. The rulers in Saigon were closely associated with French colonial rule; the rulers in Hanoi were leaders in the struggle against the French, national heroes in both the North and the South. Fourth, the routes from North to South Korea were defensible; the routes from North to South Vietnam led through neutral Laos and Cambodia, where the United States was reluctant to place troops. Fifth, in general, the geographical features of South Korea lent themselves more to the World War II-style operations, with which American commanders were familiar, than did the geography of Vietnam.

All these factors, visible in 1965, showed that war in Vietnam would be much more difficult than war in Korea, requiring a massive land war in the South and a massive air war in the North. The predictable scale of the land and air wars, conducted against politically hostile or indifferent populations, created the paradox of Vietnam that the United States never solved. The more American soldiers landed in South Vietnam, the more the Saigon regime seemed involved with foreigners. The more Saigon was involved with foreigners, the more true Vietnamese nationalists sided with the NLF. Similarly, the more American bombs fell on North Vietnam, the more the North Vietnamese felt inclined to back their government's "war against the imperialists." Thus, like Antaeus, America's opponent grew stronger each time it was smashed to the ground.

Short of the complete destruction of the material assets of North Vietnam and the imprisonment of half the population of South Vietnam, the great force of nationalism in the North and the widespread desire for social reform in the South would, sooner or later, make Vietnam a single nation once again. Even in 1965, clear-sighted people could see that the United States could not win in Vietnam. On this analysis, the principle of proportionality, which forbids the use of force where there is no chance of success, would rule against American intervention, even given the assumption that the American cause was just.

(e) Just Peace?

On 30 April 1975, North Vietnamese forces entered Saigon and renamed it Ho Chi Minh City. In 15 years of fighting, the NLF and North Vietnam had suffered perhaps 600,000 dead; the South Vietnamese supporting Saigon, 400,000; the Americans, 57,000. The landscape of Vietnam, North and South, was torn by bomb craters, devastated by herbicides, and littered with unexploded bombs, booby traps, and mines. Did the victory produce a just peace? Considering the scale of slaughter, it is hardly surprising that the victors from Hanoi dealt harshly with officials and supporters of the Saigon regime, though the great "bloodbath" predicted by defenders of American intervention did not materialize. Less excusable was Hanoi's treatment of surviving members of the NLF, very few of whom obtained positions of responsibility under the new administration in the South. Totally inexcusable was the persecution inflicted by the Hanoi government on ethnic Chinese and Vietnamese of Chinese ancestry, hundreds of thousands of whom risked their lives to flee Vietnam in the late 1970s, voting with their feet on the unacceptability of Hanoi's leadership. The arbitrary power of the landlords over the peasants had been abolished throughout Vietnam, but this seems largely to have been replaced by other arbitrary forms of power.

In seeking to throw the foreigners out of Vietnam, the North Vietnamese fought with just cause, but the victory in a just cause brought exhaustion and madness, not justice. If American intervention was unjust, it need not follow that the war against American intervention was just. Perhaps the ultimate lesson of Vietnam is that violence in war, sufficiently prolonged, perverts winners and losers alike.

11. SUGGESTIONS FOR FURTHER READING

Introduction

Some introductions to the theory of just war are Paul Ramsey, *War and the Christian Conscience* (Durham, NC: Duke University Press, 1961) and *The Just War* (New York: Scribner's 1968), James Turner Johnson, *Ideology, Reason, and Limitation of War* (Princeton, NJ: Princeton University Press, 1975), *Just War Tradition and the Restraint of War* (Princeton, NJ: Princeton University Press, 1981), and *Can Modern War Be Just?* (New Haven: Yale University Press, 1984); Michael Walzer, *Just and Unjust Wars* (New York: Basic Books, 1977); and William V. O'Brien, *The Conduct of Just and Limited War* (New York: Praeger, 1981).

Competent Authority

The text of the Second Protocol to the Fourth Geneva Convention of 1949 (U. N. Doc. A/32/144 1977) is printed in *American Journal of International Law* 66 (1978), pp. 438 ff.

Right Intention

For an analysis of the status of intentions in institutions, see Peter French, "The Corporation as a Moral Person," *American Philosophical Quarterly 16* (July, 1979). See also Patricia Werhane, *Persons, Rights, and Corporations* (Englewood Cliffs, NJ: Prentice Hall, 1983).

For a discussion of American motives in the Pacific theater of World War II, see John Dower, *War Without Mercy: Race and Power in the Pacific War* (New York: Pantheon Books, 1986).

Just Cause

For the particular difficulty Americans seem to have in distinguishing just causes from ideological crusades, see Robert W. Tucker, *The Just War* (Baltimore: Johns Hopkins University Press, 1960).

The development of the "just cause" restrictions of the U. N. Charter is described in Ruth B. Russell, *A History of the United Nations Charter* (Washington, DC: Brookings Institution, 1958). For detailed analyses of national self-defense and aggression, see Julius Stone, *Aggression and World Order* (Berkeley: University of California Press, 1958), D. W. Bowett, *Self-Defence in International Law* (Manchester: Manchester University Press, 1958); and Ian Brownlie, *International Law and the Use of Force by States* (Oxford: Clarendon Press, 1963). Careful analysis of the 1974 definition of aggression adopted by the U. N. General Assembly is given in Yehuda Melzer, *Concepts of Just War* (Leiden: Sijthoff, 1975).

Anticipation and Just Cause

Background information about the Six-Day War is in Michael Howard and Robert Hunter, *Israel and the Arab World: The Crisis of 1967* (London: Institute for Strategic Studies, 1967).

For an analysis of the initiation of the Six-Day War that differs from that given here but also ends up condoning the Israeli attack, see Walzer, *Just and Unjust Wars*.

Intervention and Just Cause

A nice discussion of the complexity of problems of intervention is Stanley Hoffman, *Duties Beyond Borders* (Syracuse, NY: Syracuse University Press, 1981). See also *Essays on Intervention*, ed. Roland J. Stanger (Columbus: Ohio State University Press, 1965); James N. Rosenau, "The Concept of Intervention," *Journal of International Affairs* 22 (1968): 165–176; R. J. Vincent, *Nonintervention and International Order* (Princeton, NJ: Princeton University Press, 1974); Ian Brownlie, "Humanitarian Intervention," in *Law and Civil War in the Modern World*, ed. John Norton Moore (Baltimore: Johns Hopkins University Press, 1974); Stephen J. Solarz, "When to Intervene," *Foreign Policy* 63 (Summer 1986): 20–39; and Jefferson McMahan, "The Ethics of Intervention," in *Political Realism and International Morality*, ed. D. Meyers and K. Kipnis (Boulder: Westview, 1987)

For a sharply critical interpretation of recent American interventionism, see Michael T. Klare, *Beyond the Vietnam Syndrome: US Interventionism in the 1980s* (Washington, DC: Institute for Policy Studies, 1981). But should readers conclude after reading Klare that the superpowers should swear off intervening in other countries' internal affairs altogether, they should ponder the notorious cases of nonintervention described in William Shawcross, *The Quality of Mercy: Cambodia, Holocaust, and Modern Conscience* (New York: Simon and Schuster, 1984); and David S. Wyman, *Abandonment of the Jews* (New York: Pantheon Books, 1984).

The Indo-Pakistani Conflict.   The Background of the Indo-Pakistani conflict is laid out in Russell Brines, *The Indo Pakistani Conflict* (London: Pall Mall, 1968); for the military narrative see Lord Carver, *War Since 1945* (New York: Putnam's 1981), Ch. 11. The war produced an apologetic literature on the Indian side, including B. M. Caul, *Confrontation with Pakistan* (Delhi: Vikas, 1971); and D. R Mankekar, *Pakistan Cut to Size* (New

Delhi: India Book Publishing, 1971). See also Thomas M. Franck and Nigel S. Rodley, "After Bangladesh: The Law of Humanitarian Intervention by Military Force," *American Journal of International Law* 62 (1973): 275–305.

Despite evidence of mass murder in East Pakistan, the United States came out against intervention and tilted against India. For a strained rationale see Henry Kissinger, *White House Years* (Boston: Little Brown, 1979).

The Osirak Raid of 1981. See Shai Feldman, "The Bombing of Osirak Revisited," *International Security* 7, no. 2 (Fall 1982): 114–142.

The Rule of Proportionality

For an analysis of the rule of proportionality, see Myres McDougal and Florentino Feliciano, *Law and Minimum World Public Order* (New Haven: Yale University Press, 1961), pp. 242 ff.

Weighing Just Cause Against Proportionality

The decisions in Belgium in 1914 are colorfully described in Barbara Tuchman, *The Guns of August* (New York: Macmillan, 1962). For the deviant view of the Russo-Finnish war advocated here, see D. F. Fleming, *The Cold War and its Origins* (Garden City, NY: Doubleday, 1961). For a discussion of what turns "extreme emergency" into a loophole in the just war doctrine, see Walzer, *Just and Unjust Wars*.

Just Outcome

For narratives of the Korean conflict, see Robert Leckie, *The Korean War* (New York: Putnam, 1962); and Barry J. Middleton, *The Compact History of the Korean War* (New York: Hawthorne Books, 1965). For a strong statement of the moral inadmissibility of Israeli occupation of territories conquered in 1967, see Edward W. Said, *The Question of Palestine* (New York: Times Books, 1979).

Jus Ad Bellum and Vietnam

For a narrative of events in the Vietnam War, See George C. Herring, *America's Longest War: The U. S. and Vietnam* (Philadelphia: Temple University Press, 1982); or Stanley Karnow, *Vietnam: A History* (New York: Viking, 1983), together with the documentary material in *The Vietnam Reader*, ed. Marcus Raskin and Bernard Fall (New York: Random House, 1965); and *Vietnam: A History in Documents*, ed. Gareth Porter (New York: New American Library, 1981). For the history of American policy, nothing surpasses the U. S. Defense Department's once-secret *Pentagon Papers*, ed. Mike Gravel (Boston: Beacon Press, 1971).

For an analysis of military tactics on the American side, see Guenter Lewy, *America in Vietnam* (New York: Oxford University Press, 1978; William Westmoreland, *A Soldier Reports* (Garden City, NY: Doubleday, 1976); Douglas Kinnard, *The War Managers* (Hanover, NH: University Press of New England, 1977), Leslie Gelb and Richard Betts, *The Irony of Vietnam: The System Worked* (Washington, DC: Brookings Institution, 1979); Harry Summers, Jr., *On Strategy: A Critical Analysis of the Vietnam War* (Novato, CA: Presidio Press, 1982); and Andrew F. Krepinevich, Jr., *The Army and Vietnam* (Baltimore: Johns Hopkins University Press, 1986). For the Vietnamese side see Vo Nguyen Giap, *Big Victory, Great Task* (London: Pall Mall, 1968), together with Robert J. O'Neill, *The Strategy of General Giap Since 1964* (Canberra: Australian National University Press, 1969).

Good background studies of the Vietnamese context include Bernard Fall, *Street Without Joy* (London: Pall Mall, 1964); G. Kahlin and John Lewis, *The United States in Vietnam* (New York: Dial Press, 1969); and, especially, Frances Fitzgerald, *Fire in the Lake* (Boston: Atlantic, Little Brown, 1972).

The U. S. State Department's legal justifications for involvement in Vietnam are "Aggression from the North: Legal Basis for United States Actions Against North Vietnam" (February 1965), reprinted in Fall and Raskin, pp. 143–155 (for criticism, see I. F. Stone, in *The Vietnam Reader*, pp. 155–164); and "The Legality of United States Participation in the Defense of Vietnam," (4 March 1966), reprinted *The Vietnam War and International Law*, ed. Richard Falk, I (Princeton, NJ: Princeton University Press, 1968). See also John Norton Moore, "The Lawfulness of Military Assistance to the Republic of Viet-Nam," *American Journal of International Law* 1-34 (1967). Arguments for the moral permissibility of American involvement in Vietnam are in William O'Brien, *The Conduct of Just and Limited War* (New York: Praeger, 1981); the stronger argument that it was morally obligatory to intervene in Vietnam is pressed by Norman Podhoretz in *Why We Were in Vietnam* (New York: Simon and Schuster, 1983).

Much criticism of American intervention of Vietnam is directed toward showing that intervention was contrary to long-term American interests; see, for example, J. W. Fulbright, *The Arrogance of Power* (New York: Random House, 1966); and Barbara Tuchman, *The March of Folly* (New York: Knopf, 1984).

The case that intervention in Vietnam was illegal is pressed by Richard A. Falk in "International Law and United States Intervention in Vietnam," *Yale Law Journal* 1051-1094 (1967); and by Charles Caumont in "A Critical Study of American Intervention in Vietnam" (1968), reprinted in *The Vietnam War and International Law*, II, ed. Richard Falk, (Princeton, NJ: Princeton University Press, 1969). The immorality of intervention from the standpoint of liberal principles is argued in George C. Herring, *America's Longest War* (New York: John Wiley, 1979); from the standpoint of human rights, in Walzer's *Just and Unjust Wars;* and from Christian ethics, in Clergy and Laity Concerned about Vietnam, *In the Name of America* (Annandale, VA: Turnpike Press, 1968). Its malevolent character is argued in Carl Oglesby and Richard Shaull, *Containment and Change* (Toronto: Macmillan, 1967); and William Shawcross, *Sideshow: Nixon, Kissinger, and the Destruction of Cambodia* (New York: Simon and Schuster, 1979).

Competent Authority.   The starting point for discussion of the competence of the Saigon regime is the Geneva accords of 1955, reprinted in *The Vietnam War and International Law*, I. For the legitimacy of the use of force by the Vietcong, see Thomas M. Franck and Nigel S. Rodely, "Legitimacy and Legal Rights of Revolutionary Movements with Special Reference to the People's Revolutionary Government of South Vietnam" (1970), reprinted in *The Vietnam War and International Law*, ed. Richard Falk, III. (Princeton, NJ: Princeton University Press, 1972). For the constitutionality of the American president's involving the United States in Vietnam without a declaration of war, see Francis Wormuth's pamphlet, "The Vietnam War: The President versus the Constitution," reprinted in *The Vietnam War and International Law*, II.

Right Intention.   For a study of intentions on the American side, see David Halberstam, *The Best and the Brightest* (New York: Random House, 1972); William Colby and Peter Forbath, *Honorable Men* (New York: Simon and Schuster, 1978); and Wallace Thies, *When Governments Collide: Coercion and Diplomacy in the Vietnam Conflict 1964–68* (Berkeley: University of California Press, 1980). For the intentions of the war's principal architect, see Lyndon B. Johnson, *The Vantage Point* (New York: Holt, Rinehart, and Winston, 1971).

Just Cause.   The incidents in 1964 in the Gulf of Tonkin are recounted in Joseph C. Goulden, *Truth is the First Casualty: The Gulf of Tonkin Affair—Illusion and Reality* (Chicago: Rand McNally, 1969); and Eugene Windchy, *Tonkin Gulf* (Garden City, NY: Doubleday, 1971).

Proportionality.   O'Brien's discussion of proportionality in the Vietnam war is in *The Conduct of Just and Limited War*, Ch. 5; see also Eliot Hawkins, "An Approach to Issues of International Law Raised by United States Conduct in Vietnam," in *The Vietnam War and International Law*, I. The immense difficulties of carrying out the American program were described by the pro-NLF journalist Wilfrid Burchett in *Vietnam: The Inside Story of a Guerrilla War* (New York: International Publishers, 1965) and ignored by American policy makers who thought they knew better. The costs imposed on Vietnam by American military methods are detailed in Jonathan Schell, *The Military Half* (New York: Knopf, 1968).

Just Peace.   A book that captures the ironies of the Vietnam denouement in achingly personal terms in Truong Nhu Tang, *A Vietcong Memoir* (New York: Random House, 1985).

4

JUST WAR THEORY II

How to Fight

1. INTRODUCTION

People who believe that there are moral limits defining *when* wars should be
fought naturally believe that there are moral limits defining *how* they
should be fought. The idea that there are right and wrong ways to conduct
war is an ancient one. In the Hebrew Bible, God states that though it may
be necessary to kill one's enemy, it is never permissible to cut down his fruit
trees (Deut. 20:19). In the sixth century B.C. the Hindu Laws of Manu
specified, "When the King fights with his foes in battle, let him not strike
with weapons concealed in wood, nor with barbed, poisoned, or flaming
arrows."

Over the centuries, a vast array of rules and customs constituting *jus
in bello* have been elaborated. There are rules that specify proper behavior
toward neutral countries, toward the citizens of neutral countries, and
toward neutral ships. There are rules governing what can and cannot be
done to enemy civilians, to enemy soldiers on the battlefield, and to enemy
soldiers when they are wounded and when they have surrendered. There
are rules concerning proper and improper weapons of war, and proper
and improper tactics on the battlefield.

In the late nineteenth and twentieth centuries, many of these "laws of
war" were codified in a series of treaties, conventions, and protocols, signed

and ratified by most of the principal nations of the world. Nations ratifying these sets of rules undertook to impose them on their own military establishments, pledging to prosecute violations and punish wrongdoers. When domestic enforcements have fallen short, nations victorious in war have undertaken the prosecution of violations perpetrated by defeated enemies. (Victorious nations are rarely prosecuted.)

With the exceptions of the Geneva Convention banning chemical warfare (1925) and the Second Protocol to the Fourth Geneva Convention (1977), the United States has ratified most of the principal international conventions regarding the laws of war. In their field manuals, the various military services of the United States consider themselves bound by the Hague Conventions of 1899 and 1907, by the Geneva Conventions of 1929, and by the four Geneva Conventions of 1949, which govern the sick and wounded on the battlefield (I), the sick and wounded at sea (II), prisoners of war (III), and the protection of civilian persons in time of war (IV).

2. NECESSITY, PROPORTIONALITY, AND DISCRIMINATION

For the student approaching the laws of war for the first time, the profusion of covenants, treaties, customs, and precedents can be bewildering. But fortunately there are a few leading ideas that have governed the development of the laws of war. The first is that the destruction of life and property, even enemy life and property, is inherently bad. It follows that military forces should cause no more destruction than is strictly necessary to achieve their objectives. (Notice that the principle does not say that whatever is necessary is permissible, but that everything permissible must be necessary.) This is the principle of necessity: that *wanton* destruction is forbidden. More precisely, the principle of necessity specifies that a military operation is forbidden if there is some alternative operation that causes less destruction but has the same probability of producing a successful military result.

The second leading idea is that the amount of destruction permitted in pursuit of a military objective must be proportionate to the importance of the objective. This is the *military* principle of proportionality (which must be distinguished from the *political* principle of proportionality in the *jus ad bellum*). It follows from the military principle of proportionality that certain objectives should be ruled out of consideration on the grounds that too much destruction would be caused in obtaining them.

The third leading idea, the principle of noncombatant immunity, is that civilian life and property should not be subjected to military force: military force must be directed only at military objectives. Obviously, the principle of noncombatant immunity is useful only if there is a consensus about what counts as "civilian" and what counts as "military." In the older Hague Conventions, a list of explicit nonmilitary targets is developed:

"buildings dedicated to religion, art, science, or charitable purposes, historic monuments, hospitals . . . undefended towns, buildings, or dwellings."Anything that is not explicitly mentioned qualifies as a military target. But this list is overly restrictive, and the consensus of modern thought takes "military" targets to include servicemen, weapons, and supplies; the ships and vehicles that transport them; and the factories and workers that produce them. Anything that is not "military" is "civilian." Since, on either definition, the principle of noncombatant immunity distinguishes acceptable military objectives from unacceptable civilian objectives, it is often referred to as the principle of discrimination. (In the morality of war, discrimination is good, not evil.)

There is an objective and subjective version of the principle of noncombatant immunity. The objective version holds that if civilians are killed as a result of military operations, the principle is violated. The subjective version holds that if civilians are *intentionally* killed as a result of military operations, the principle is violated. The interpretation of "intentional" in the subjective version is disputed, but the general idea is that the killing of civilians is intentional if, and only if, they are the chosen *targets* of military force. It follows, on the subjective version, that if civilians are killed in the course of a military operation directed at a military target, the principle of discrimination has *not* been violated. Obviously, the objective version of the principle of discrimination is far more restrictive than the subjective.

The earlier Hague Conventions leaned toward the objective version of the principle of discrimination. The later Geneva Convention (IV), as interpreted in the Second Protocol of 1977, leans toward the subjective version:

> The civilian population as such, as well as individual civilians, shall not be the object of attack. . . . Indiscriminate attacks are prohibited, [including] those which are not directed at a specific military objective, those which employ a method or means which cannot be directed at a specific objective, or those which employ a method or means the effects of which cannot be limited or which are of a nature to strike military objectives and civilians or civilian objects without distinction.

If we adopt the subjective version of the principle of discrimination, it does not follow that any number of civilians may be permissibly killed so long as they are killed in pursuit of military objectives. The number of civilian deaths resulting from a military operation remains limited by the principle of proportionality. In sum,

> In all military operations, civilians should not be the target of attack. The deaths of civilians or damage to their property which are side-effects of military operations must be necessary for the achievement of the objective and proportionate to its importance.

The principles of necessity, proportionality, and discrimination apply with equal force to all sides in war. Violation of the rules cannot be justified or excused on the grounds that one is fighting on the side of justice. Those who developed the laws of war learned through experience that just causes must have moral limits.

3. PHILOSOPHICAL RATIONALES FOR THE LAWS OF WAR

The three principles described above are accepted by most contemporary governments and military establishments. For the philosopher seeking a theory of just war, acceptance of the principles is not enough. The philosopher wants to determine whether there is some underlying moral rationale behind the rules. What is the relationship between the laws of war and the principles of morality? Does the current list of laws exhaust the moral aspects of combat? Do those laws morally bind soldiers and officers? If they do, how do they bind, and how strongly, and under what circumstances? There are almost as many answers as there are moral theories.

(a) Are the Laws of War Mere Conventions?

A radical—but popular—approach to the moral content of the laws of war maintains that these laws are mere conventions. The claim that the rules of *jus in bello* are "conventional" implies that the rules are not derived from divine commands, like the Ten Commandments, or from natural features of human life, like the principles of Aristotle's ethics. If the rules are conventions, they result from voluntary acts and agreements of human beings, acts and agreements that, without significant loss to the parties involved, might have been differently made.

Often a convention arises as a solution to a certain sort of social problem called a "coordination problem." Consider, for example, the problem of getting around by car. It is to everyone's advantage if all cars going in the same direction stay on the same side of the road, but there is no divine law or natural feature that indicates whether cars should drive on the right or drive on the left. A designated traffic authority solves the problem by simply *deciding* whether cars should drive on the left or drive on the right, and there is no point in discussing whether the authority made the right decision or the wrong one. Some commentators on the laws of war have argued that the laws of war are like the rules of the road: conventions that allow nations to pursue military objectives with greater efficiency than would be possible if there were no laws of war.

The question of whether the laws of war are merely conventional, or more than conventional, is not just a philosopher's puzzle. If the laws are merely conventional, it follows that unilateral violations of the law are not the highest form of wickedness, and may be easily justifiable if one is demonstrably fighting for a just cause. If the laws are merely conventional, one is not bound to keep the rules when fighting against opponents who consistently ignore them. If the principle of noncombatant immunity is a mere convention, then should your enemy take *your* civilians as targets, you would be a fool not to take *their* civilians as targets, if it would be a military plus for you to do so. It is neither moral nor rational to drive steadily on the right if all other cars constantly drive pell-mell. If the laws of war are conventions designed to produce efficiency through coordination, then the most that can be said for their binding character is that each nation is obliged, in the course of war, not to be the *first* to break the rules. The British in 1939 were inclined not to take German cities as bombing targets, but after the Germans bombed London on 24 August 1940, British airmen struck Berlin the following night, citing the German attack as a justifying precedent.

Certain features of the history of the laws of war do suggest a conventional character for these rules. A good part of what is considered acceptable behavior in peacetime has remained constant from classical times, but what is considered acceptable behavior in war has changed radically over the centuries. This mutable character of war regulations smacks of convention. Furthermore, the bulk of the current rules have been laboriously worked out by hundreds of delegates in international congresses. It seems implausible that all these delegates have been slowly *discovering* the true laws of war, and far more plausible that the delegates have been *inventing* laws that gain their validity solely from their acceptability to nation-states. Finally, there are many rules of war—for example, the identification of medical vehicles with a red cross—that are indubitably conventional: no one would be harmed if it were decided to mark medical vehicles with green crosses.

Despite this evidence, there are reasons for thinking that many of the laws of war are not mere conventions. When working within a system of conventions, it is usually not to one's advantage, and not to anyone's advantage, to adhere to the conventions when no one else does. But in the case of the laws of war, it is often no disadvantage to keep to the rules even when the other side does not. Suppose, for example, that the enemy has started killing (or starving) their prisoners of war. It does not follow that it is to your advantage to start killing prisoners, who may be able to work as part of your war effort, and lives are saved if you do not. Though no good is produced if you drive steadily on the right when everyone drives pell-mell, some good is produced if you do not kill your prisoners when the other side does.

Nation-states often complain that they are placed at a disadvantage if they keep to the laws of war and their enemies do not. These complaints, though common, are very rarely justified. When the Germans bombed

Rotterdam, and then London, Coventry, and other British cities in the blitz, they violated the principle of noncombatant immunity. It does not follow that the British would have been at a disadvantage if they had not bombed Berlin in 1940. The bombing of Berlin obtained no military objective; its purpose was to satisfy the British desire for revenge. Since good can come from unilateral adherence to the laws of war, the logic of the laws of war does not correspond to the logic of a system of conventions.

If we reject the idea that the laws of war are mere conventions, we can assume that they have moral content sufficient to bind nations independently of what other nations do. But we still have no theory of the relationship between war laws and moral laws.

(b) The Laws of War as Promises

Perhaps the simplest account of the relationship between the laws of war and the principles of morality is the view that the laws of war bind nations morally if, and only if, they have promised to keep them. The Hague and Geneva Conventions, mentioned above, have all been ratified by the U.S. Senate. Through ratification, the United States has promised to obey these rules, and since nations are morally obliged to keep their promises, the United States is morally obliged to obey the rules. The same goes for other nations that have signed and ratified these international covenants.

This "promise theory" links the rules of *jus in bello* to the principles of morality in a particularly vivid way. If there are any moral rules at all, the rule that one ought to keep promises is surely one of them. But this approach to the laws of war has some disturbing consequences.

It follows from the promise approach that if a nation has *not* signed any of the international convenants, it has no moral obligation to obey any of the laws of war. This implies, for example, that North Korean treatment of American prisoners of war during the Korean conflict, which involved considerable physical brutality as well as the psychological tortures of brainwashing, cannot be criticized as morally wrong because the North Korean government had not signed the Third Geneva Convention of 1949, which forbids "cruel treatment, torture . . . outrages upon personal dignity, and humiliating and degrading treatment" of prisoners of war. In normal circumstances, we feel that it is immoral to torture people, and that to inflict intense suffering and misery on physically helpless people who lie within one's power is a mark of sadistic character. There is no reason to think we should feel any differently about such acts when they occur in the abnormal circumstances of war, or when they are performed by soldiers of nations who have not signed on the dotted line.

In general, then, nations and their military forces may be morally bound by rules even if they have made no prior agreement to keep them.

To some degree, American military practice acknowledges this: the 1976 edition of the U.S. Army manual on the law of land warfare commits the Army, with some qualifications, to adherence to the 1925 Geneva Protocol for the Prohibition of Poisonous Gases and Bacteriological Methods of Warfare, even though this Protocol has never been ratified by the U.S. Senate.

The promise approach also implies that nations ratifying international covenants have a special obligation to keep to the rules even when the enemy does not, and even if there is some military disadvantage in keeping to the agreements. Consider two nations, A and B. Suppose that A has ratified the Geneva Protocols and B has not, that A and B are engaged in a desperate struggle, and that each side has adopted the expedient of taking no prisoners on the battlefield. According to the promise approach, A has done something reprehensible that B has not done, namely, broken its promises. But since each side is doing the same thing, intuitively their actions seem equally reprehensible or equally acceptable.

Examples like these indicate that the whole story of the moral content of the laws of war cannot be discovered in the idea of a public promise.

(c) The Laws of War and Utilitarianism

In our discussion of *jus ad bellum*, we developed a revised rule of proportionality specifying that it is permissible to use force to secure one's rights unless the use of force brings considerably more evil than good into the world. The qualification about "good and evil" introduces a utilitarian dimension into just war theory: not the standard utilitarianism that says it is always permissible to adopt a policy that produces more good than evil (compared with the alternatives), but an attenuated utilitarianism that insists it is always wrong to adopt a policy that produces *much* more evil than good (compared with the alternatives).

It follows that if a nation is to pursue its rights in a morally permissible way, it must keep the destructiveness of its military strategies to a level consistent with the utilitarian rule. The principles of necessity and military proportionality, and all the rules of war derived from these principles, obtain their moral content from the utilitarian conception that it is wrongful to destroy the good things of the world, even good things belonging to enemies that are waging unjust wars. Since the utilitarian code generates unconditional obligations, which bind regardless of what others do, it follows on this interpretation that the rules of proportionality and necessity bind nations, even in conflicts with states that neither acknowledge nor obey the rules of war.

At this point a radical difference between the rules of necessity and proportionality and the rule of discrimination reveals itself. The utilitarian rationale, so natural for the rules of necessity and military proportionality, fails to explain or justify the rule of discrimination. Discrimination requires that noncombatants should *never* be chosen targets of attack, *even if* considerably more good than evil could be produced by choosing civilian targets. Suppose military commanders have an important objective that is equally likely to be achieved by strategy A and strategy B, that strategy A requires that civilians be chosen as targets *and* that about 1,000 enemy civilians will die in the attack, that strategy B refuses to take civilians as targets *but* about 10,000 enemy soldiers will die in the attack, and that no other strategies have any chance of success. According to the principle of discrimination, strategy A is unacceptable, despite the fact that considerably more evil than good results from strategy B. For this principle, only non-utilitarian justifications will do.

(d) Noncombatant Immunity and Chivalry

Historically, the idea of noncombatant immunity developed in the High Middle Ages, as part of the medieval traditions of chivalry. Chivalry presented the ideal of the virtuous knight: courageous in battle, fair with enemies, compassionate toward the weak. To act in violation of the principle of discrimination was to use force contrary to chivalrous virtues. It takes no courage to kill women and children, and little more to kill an enemy who has laid down his arms. The moral content of the principle of discrimination, on this account, consists in the fact that respect for noncombatant immunity is a mark of virtuous character.

But the historical connection between chivalry and noncombatant immunity cannot, by itself, show that respect for noncombatant immunity is morally required. Since good moral character is something that is possible for each and is required of all, the moral quality of chivalrous virtues can be established only by demonstrating that everyone is morally obliged to be a knight—and that demonstration cannot be supplied. The military commander who adopts strategy A in the example above and orders an attack on civilians may not be a white knight, but it is not clear that morality obliges him to be a white knight when faced with the choice between A and B. Certainly chivalrousness is a virtue, but it is not obviously a *moral* virtue. It is a mark of genuine moral virtues that people of good character act not only in accordance with moral virtues but also for the sake of them: the just man does just things, and does them because they are just. It would be perverse, in analyzing twentieth-century wars, to say that soldiers are placed on the battlefield for the purpose of exhibiting chivalry.

Other features of war, particularly modern war, differ from the knightly setting so sharply as to undercut the applicability of chivalrous concepts. Medieval knights, at least in legend, fought each other on roughly equal terms, one on one, with similar equipment. In all wars from antiquity to the present, victory is usually obtained by a side with the unequal advantage: the side with the larger phalanx, the more men engaged in the "push of the pike," the larger cavalry, the bigger guns. In contemporary war, men in tanks and armored vehicles and bombers kill men not in tanks or armored vehicles or bombers. The idea of courage in equal combat is largely absent in these situations: the bomber pilot and tank commander take risks on occasion, but on many other occasions they kill in battle with little risk to themselves; the same is true of men in the artillery and those engaged in laying mines. The guerrilla leader who overwhelms an isolated outpost, or the field commander who sends a battalion against a company, is not fighting fair by knightly standards. From this we should infer not that contemporary war is wicked, but that the knightly standards are irrelevant.

(e) Direct and Indirect Killing

The principle of noncombatant immunity is linked in the rules of war with the principle of combatant *non*immunity: It is never permissible to take civilians as targets, but it is always permissible to take combatants as targets, at least until they lay down their arms. As we have seen in our discussion of pacifism, rationalizing this moral vulnerability of soldiers is more difficult than it first seems. The commonest justification for killing—self-defense—rarely applies, and the usual excuses—ignorance and coercion—are rarely applicable; soldiers can almost always aim to miss, or surrender rather than kill the enemy. The idea that civilians are "innocent" and soldiers are "guilty" collapses before the modern facts that civilians in democracies often demand that national leaders declare war, whereas soldiers often do their best to avoid shedding blood: American military commanders after World War II were amazed to discover that 50 percent of American combat troops had not fired their rifles even once. Furthermore, it cannot be argued that the killing of soldiers is justifiable because the killing serves the cause of justice, since the permissibility of killing soldiers is extended by the laws of war to the just and the unjust side alike.

To keep the principle of discrimination afloat, just war theorists sometimes introduce a distinction between *direct* killing and *indirect* killing. In direct killing, death is the intended goal of an act, or an intended means to an intended goal; in indirect killing, death is a side effect caused by an act that has some other intended goal. Given the distinction, theorists declare that the direct killing of civilians in war is always murder; the indirect killing of civilians in the course of military operations aimed at military objectives is regrettable but not murderous.

The distinction between direct killing and indirect killing, between death as a means or end and death as a side effect, is not a distinction recognized in the ordinary criminal law. In domestic society, if I freely perform an action that I know will result in the death of an innocent person, I am a murderer, regardless of whether the death of that person was my main goal or merely a side effect of my search for something else. If the victim has a right to life, that right is just as much violated if he is killed indirectly as it is violated if he is killed directly. Why, then, should we accept the just war theorist's verdict that military commanders who undertake operations they know will produce civilian deaths as side effects are not murderers, when we would condemn their acts as murder if the perpetrators were not in uniform?

Defenders of the idea of noncombatant immunity will argue that although the distinction between direct killing and indirect killing has no status in criminal law, it has no status for the technical reason that judges and juries simply cannot look into people's souls, determine their goals, and infer from this assessment of goals whether their acts of killing are direct or indirect. But this legal situation should not blind us—so the argument goes—to the moral distinction between direct killing and indirect killing.

The moral distinction between direct killing and indirect killing will be clear only if the logical distinction between direct killing and indirect killing is clear. But does the distinction between direct killing and indirect killing make sense? The distinction between *death as a means* and *death as a side effect* is fine indeed. Normally, we say that M is a "means" to goal G if, in normal conditions, the production of M guarantees the existence of G, that is, if M in normal conditions is a sufficient condition of G. But the side effect S produced in the course of getting G may be so closely connected with G that, in normal conditions, we can have S only if we also have G. This makes G a necessary condition for S, and S a sufficient condition for G! What, then, is the difference between a means and a side effect?

Consider the analysis of direct versus indirect killing as it is applied by Catholic moral theologians to problems involving abortion. Pregnant mother A is diagnosed as having cancer of the uterus; if a hysterectomy is performed, the cancer may be caught before it spreads. According to Catholic theologians, the hysterectomy is permissible even though the fetus will surely die, because the death of the fetus is a side effect of the struggle against cancer. Pregnant mother B is having a difficult pregnancy caused by problems with the fetus; unless an abortion is performed, she may die before her pregnancy comes to term. In this case, the theologians declare that the abortion is impermissible because the death of the fetus is the means of removing the threat to the mother. But in either case the fetus dies, and in normal circumstances this suffices to save the mother. The reader is free to determine whether the moral difference between case A and case B is as clear as defenders of the distinction between direct and indirect killing believe. But if we cannot distinguish morally between direct and indirect killing, the principle of noncombatant immunity is incoherent.

These observations show that the principle of noncombatant immunity, the principle that students of war like Michael Walzer consider the central "war convention," is much more difficult to justify and explain than the principles of necessity and proportionality. It should come as no surprise that the principle of noncombatant immunity has been, in this century, the most frequently violated of all the principles of *jus in bello.*

4. THE CASE OF STRATEGIC BOMBING

(a) The Air Power Theorists

One of the reasons that noncombatant immunity has had such a hard time of it in the twentieth century is that the twentieth century has been the century of strategic bombing.

Theories about the military usefulness of strategic bombing—the use of bombers to strike deep in enemy territory, beyond any point held by ground forces—were promulgated by a number of authors in the years immediately following World War I. The war had been a catastrophe for the winners (5 million killed) as well as the losers (3.3 million killed), and all postwar strategic thinkers were urgently concerned that the next war be different from the war just past.

The great casualties of World War I resulted from the unexpected length of the war and the overwhelming dominance of defense over offense, which led to a stable front and the agony of the trenches. The remedy, then, lay in designing offenses that would dominate defense and make war short. For Basil Liddell-Hart and J. C. F. Fuller, the solution was tanks, motorized infantry, and tactical air support. For Jan Smuts, Giulio Douhet, Hugh Trenchard, and J. M. Spaight, the remedy was air warfare in general and strategic bombing in particular. But what was to be bombed, and to what end?

Given the planes and equipment available in the 1920s, the logical targets for bombers were the cities of the enemy. As Maj. Oliver Stewart wrote in 1925, a bomber "can hit a town from ten thousand feet—if the town is big enough" (Lee Kennett, *A History of Strategic Bombing*, p. 49). The early theorists made a virtue of necessity and declared that towns and cities were the ideal targets for the new short war that was to replace the war of the trenches. The scale and effects of the air offensive attack were described by Douhet: 300 bombers, equipped with gas bombs, could kill 10,000 people in each of 10 cities in a single day: "the only salvation will be in caves" (Kennett, p. 56). The great air offensive would soon kill 10 percent of the enemy population "and bring the other 90 percent to its knees."

Douhet published these nightmares in *The Command of the Air* in 1921, creating a storm of controversy. In 1923, a conference met at The Hague to establish "rules of aerial warfare" that would prevent Douhet's views from seizing hold. The rules included

Art. 22: Aerial bombardment for the purpose of terrorizing the civilian population . . . is prohibited; . . .

Art. 24: Aerial bombardment is legitimate only when directed at a military objective . . . the bombardment of cities, towns, villages, dwellings, or buildings not in the immediate neighborhood of the operations of land forces is prohibited.

These rules, if adopted, would have condemned not only the bombing possible in 1923, but most of the bombing of World War II. But the rules were not adopted for a variety of reasons, among them the fact that the national air forces, fighting for recognition from the traditional services, did not want a set of rules that would crimp their wings in the next big war.

The condemnation of city bombardment in the Hague rules of 1923 did not deter the apostles of strategic bombing. Douhet's air attack was a nightmare vision, but the great battles of World War I—Verdun and the Somme and Passchendaele—were nightmare *memories*. If the war was short, the number of casualties would be far less than the number that fell in and between the trenches. The same utilitarian moral thrust that supported the principles of necessity and proportionality supported the plan for the air offensive. Spaight wrote in 1924:

However intense the fighting in the air, the slaughter will be as nothing compared with that of the older war . . . . (*Air Power and War Rights*, p. 4) Properly trained and directed [air power] is capable of transforming the whole face of war almost beyond recognition. It can turn the old, crude, hideous, blood letting business into an almost bloodless surgery of forcible international adjustment, to the immeasurable advantage of mankind . . . mass slaughter lies buried, one hopes, in the war cemeteries of France and Flanders. (*Air Power and War Rights*, p. 2)

The hitch was that the victims of trench warfare were almost all soldiers, while the victims of air warfare would almost all be civilians.

The apostles of air warfare could not remain silent about the Hague rules, which embodied the distinction between direct and indirect killing, nor about the chivalric tradition of noncombatant immunity. Douhet declared the tradition obsolete.

Any distinction between belligerents and nonbelligerents is no longer admissible today either in fact or theory. Not in theory because when nations are at war, everyone takes part in it: the soldier carrying his gun, the woman loading shells in the factory, the farmer growing wheat, the scientist experimenting in his laboratory. Not in fact because nowadays the offensive may reach anyone, and it begins to look now as though the safest place may be the trenches. (*Command of the Air*, p. 195)

Spaight likewise took noncombatant immunity head-on, and argued that war is not a contest of armies but a contest of states:

It is a question, first and last, of persuading minds—the minds of the government and (because governments in all modern states are servants of the people) of the people of the enemy country. . . . It has never been possible to dispense with the preliminary trials of strength between the opposing armies or fleets before the ultimate task, the exertion of the necessary forcible pressure upon the enemy government and people, could be approached . . . now, for the first time, it has become possible to dispense with the preliminary stages. Air power can strike straight at the heart of the enemy state. . . . It will not waste time on the slaughter of people who are only the armed instruments of the sovereign people of the enemy nation. (*Air Power and War Rights*, p. 3)

Air warfare and democracy stand tradition on its head: now the civilians are guilty and the soldiers are innocent.

Spaight's argument from the collective responsibility of modern nation-states to the guilt of whole populations is a neat rejoinder to scruples about noncombatant immunity, but few today will be persuaded by it, if for no other reason than that strategic bombing kills children who have no right to vote. (Spaight put so little faith in his own argument that he proposed plans for *joint* evacuations of cities in future air wars: "I will give you property to destroy if you give me life to save.") The better argument for strategic bombing is the utilitarian one: Why stick with noncombatant immunity when doing so will not save lives but lose them? But for the utilitarian argument to be effective, there must be some demonstration that the bomber offensive will work.

Douhet offered no evidence beyond his own rough rhetoric that the air offensive would create such terror that no nation could withstand it. Spaight carefully assembled evidence of civilian panic in cities subjected to strategic bombing: "No one who is acquainted with the facts can admit that the masses of people who left London [during the bombing of 1917] were exclusively 'Jews and aliens'" (*Air Power and War Rights*, p. 9)—as the British patriotic press had claimed. Thus, in the next war "No amount of composure, no surplusage of bull-dog tenacity, can save a people raided copiously, scientifically, systematically . . . (*Air Power and War Rights*, p. 13). For in the next war, unlike World War I, the air attack would be "no longer a side show."

But this anecdotal data about the small-scale bomber offensives of World War I could scarcely demonstrate that strategic bombing would bring swift victory in a major war. The advocates of air power took its success on faith, and the public accepted their case. The peoples of Europe came to believe that the next war would destroy the capitals of the continent in a few days. For the theorists, even this was better than going back to the trenches.

(b) The British Bomber Offensive Against Germany

In the months following September 1939, both Britain and Germany attempted to keep their air forces within the guidelines set down at The Hague in 1923. The first attack that clearly flouted the rules was the German attack on Rotterdam (14 May 1940), which left 1,000 Dutch civilians dead and was described by the Nazis as a reprisal for an alleged British attack on Freiburg. The British responded by attacking oil depots and railroads along the Ruhr, and they continued these attacks on quasi-military objectives through 1940 and 1941.

The British airmen soon discovered that striking specific ground targets was a strenuous business. Night navigation was difficult (one British airplane bombed *Liverpool*), fighter resistance was unexpectedly stiff, and the attrition rate was so severe that a full tour of duty amounted practically to a death sentence. When the Germans commenced bombing England in August 1940, they faced all these problems plus superior British radar. The Hague rules went out the window, and the Luftwaffe shifted to attacks on British cities, destroying Coventry in November 1940 and central London in December.

All through 1940 and 1941 the British Air Ministry kept its bombers flying to specified targets. "In no circumstances should night bombing be allowed to degenerate into mere indiscriminate action, which is contrary to the policy of His Majesty's government," read a typical directive (Max Hastings, *Bomber Command*, p. 100). Many German civilians were dying in the raids, but the Air Staff Vice Chief, Sir Richard Peirse, believed that these casualties were acceptable, and only acceptable, on the grounds that they (in the words of the official British government historians) "remained a by-product of the primary intention to hit a military target" (Charles Webster and Noble Frankland, *The Strategic Air Offensive Against Germany*, I, p. 154).

As we have seen, the distinction between a means to an end and a foreseen by-product is a fine one, but it took all of 1941 to break it down. At the end of 1941, it was clear that the British Bomber Command had suffered terrible losses, with no apparent effect on the German war effort. One-third of British war production had been devoted to the bomber offensive, production that could be shifted to support other dimensions of the war effort. The neat sets of German targets developed at Command headquarters outside London took on an air of absurdity when it was discovered (in August 1941) that less than one-third of British aircraft were dropping their bombs within five miles of their objectives.

According to the official historians, the choice for the RAF in January 1942 was between area bombing and no bombing at all. Churchill reached a decision, and on 14 February, the die was cast: "It has been decided that the primary objective for [Bomber Command] operations should be focused on the morale of the enemy civilian population, and in particular, of the industrial workers." On 20 February, Churchill found the perfect instrument for the new campaign: Sir Arthur Harris.

Though the new policy of area bombing was not publicly announced, the British public could infer from war reports that targeting policy had changed, and a policy debate ensued. The British critics, few but articulate, staked their case against the bomber offensive on the principle of noncombatant immunity. In Parliament, Richard Stokes challenged: "Is the Rt Honorable Air Minister aware that a growing volume of opinion in this country considers indiscriminate bombing of civilian centers both morally wrong and strategic lunacy?" (Max Hastings, *Bomber Command*, p. 192). A lobby group calling itself The Bombing Restriction Committee distributed leaflets in London headed STOP BOMBING CIVILIANS. George Bell, bishop of Chichester, rose in the House of Lords to argue:

> I desire to challenge the government on the policy which directs the bombing of enemy towns on the present scale, especially with reference to civilians who are noncombatants . . . the Allies stand for something greater than power. . . . It is of supreme importance that we . . . should so use power that it is always under the control of law. (Max Hastings, *Bomber Command*, p. 199)

The Air Ministry respected these arguments sufficently to spend the whole war engaged in public deception about British targeting policy, maintaining year after year that civilian deaths were side effects of military operations. Air crews assembling for bombing raids were told that Darmstadt was "a center of the pharmaceutical industry," that Dresden was "an industrial city of first-class importance," and so forth—descriptions that would have astonished the residents of those cities, who were in fact the actual targets. What the Air Ministry really believed, if the official historians' attitude is typical, was that the distinction between means-to-an-end and side-effects was meaningless, and that concern about the combatant/noncombatant distinction was wildly inappropriate when dealing with an enemy who had killed 40,000 British civilians in the blitz, which Hitler had begun 19 months before the British area-bombing policy was adopted. Harris was particularly unmoved by complaints of civilian casualties:

> The point is often made that bombing is specially wicked because it causes casualties among civilians. This is true, but then all wars have caused casualties among civilians. After the last war, it was estimated that our blockade of German had caused nearly 800,000 deaths—naturally these were mainly of woman and children and old people because at all costs the enemy had had to keep his fighting men adequately fed. This was a death rate much in excess of even the most ruthless exponents of air frightfulness. . . . Even in more civilized times of today the siege of cities, accompanied by the bombardment of the city as a whole, is still normal practice, and in no circumstances were women and children allowed to pass out of the city, because their presence in it and their consumption of food would inevitably hasten the end of the siege (*Bomber Offensive* pp. 176–77).
> There was nothing to be ashamed of, except in the sense that everybody might be ashamed of the sort of thing that has to be done in every war, as of war itself (*Bomber Offensive* p. 58).

What is remarkable about this moral debate is that the wrangle about innocent civilians, side-effects, and primary intentions virtually preempted reference to the other, perhaps better grounded, moral principles of war—

necessity and proportionality—principles at least as relevant to evaluating the bomber offensive as the principle of discrimination.

For example, was the bombing offensive *necessary* for victory? What were the alternatives? Surely the choice was not between "area bombing" and "nothing." The British could have continued to seek out military targets, taking advantage of the new bombsights and navigational aids to obtain greater accuracy. They could have transferred bombers to the North Atlantic and the Middle East, assisting Navy and Army campaigns. They could have attempted to retool the bomber factories to produce more fighters, and military equipment of other kinds. They could have opened up a second front in Normandy in 1942 or 1943, instead of 1944.

Did Churchill and Secretary of State Sinclair have any reason to believe that the bomber offensive would bring victory and that none of these other alternatives could? Before the war, it was widely believed that massive bombardment could break civilian morale. But by 1942, the British had firsthand evidence that massive bombing would not crush morale, since the onslaught of the Luftwaffe had failed to do this in 1940 and 1941. Churchill himself wrote, "It is disputable whether bombing by itself will be a decisive factor in the present war. All we have learnt since the war began shows that its effects, both physical and moral, are greatly exaggerated" (Max Hastings, *Bomber Command*, p. 132).

So the men who chose to have area bombing could not base their case on necessity. What about proportionality? Did the contribution of the bomber offensive to victory, compared with the alternatives, justify its cost in lives? Consider just one of the alternatives: the opening of a second front in Normandy in 1942 or 1943. By engaging the enemy directly in a vital area, the British would have put far greater stress on the German war-making machine than they produced with the bomber offensive, and Churchill knew this. The war might have ended sooner, saving not only many German civilians' lives but many lives, perhaps millions of lives, on the eastern front. Why then, did Churchill favor the bomber offensive over a second front in Europe?

To be sure, the invasion of Europe might not succeed: Churchill, the architect of the disastrous amphibious invasion at Gallipoli in 1915, felt this perhaps too keenly. But the bomber offensive, just like the second front, was something that might not succeed, might not justify its losses with results. The decisive argument against the second front, never publicly avowed, was that a land invasion would lose mainly British and American lives while saving mainly Russian and German lives. In the moral calculations of Churchill and Harris, a British life counted for more than a Russian life or a German life. Harris wrote in a private letter in 1945, "I would not regard the whole of the remaining cities in Germany as worth the bones of one British grenadier" (Hastings, *Bomber Command*, p. 402). Compared with a second front in France in 1943, the bomber offensive was good for Britain but bad for humanity. On this view, the British bomber offensive violated the principle of proportionality, for the laws of war are without nationality.

From February 1942 to May 1945, the Allied air offensive destroyed 3.7 million German homes and killed 593,000 German civilians, 80,000 or more in the city of Dresden on the single night of 12 February 1945. The destruction of Dresden provoked sufficient revulsion in England to give even Churchill pause: "We shall not be able to get housing materials out of Germany for our own needs because some temporary provision [will] have to be made for the Germans themselves" (Hastings, *Bomber Command*, p. 401). Harris was less moved. "The feeling over Dresden could be easily explained by any psychiatrist," he wrote. "It is connected with German bands and Dresden shepherdesses."

(c) American Bombing and Hiroshima

American B-17s joined the British bomber offensive over Germany in January 1943. Like the British in 1939, the Americans were committed to daylight precision bombing, and like the British they soon discovered that precision bombing was easier described than done: the famed Norden bombsight failed to function in bad weather; fighter opposition was fierce (German fighters shot down 148 American bombers in a single week in 1943); and German war production kept on increasing right into 1944. By the time the Americans implemented a plan that really hurt the German war effort—massive precision attacks on the German synthetic fuel industry (May-August 1944)—most of the top leaders had lost faith in the military usefulness of precision bombing. When winter weather arrived, the oil effort was broken off. By February 1945, the Americans had thoroughly succumbed to the British system of terror raids on cities.

In June 1944, the first B-29 raid on Japan seemed to confirm the European experience: about 100 planes attacked but failed to damage the steelworks at Yawata. Numerous precision raids through 1944 were foiled by clouds and wind. In January and February 1945, the Army Air Forces, after some in-service protests, began small incendiary raids on Japanese cities at night. On 9 March, not quite a month after Dresden, the new commander of bombing operations, Curtis LeMay, launched 334 B-29s on an incendiary night raid against Tokyo. A great wave of fire swept the city, and by morning at least 84,000 people were dead.

Unlike the Dresden raid, the burning of Tokyo inspired no protests on the home front. Between March and August 1945, LeMay and his B-29s attacked and burned nearly every city in Japan, while American fighters flew virtually unopposed across the countryside, attacking trains and bridges and occasionally strafing the roads. After American forces captured Iwo Jima and Okinawa, the Japanese government formed a people's volunteer corps to defend the homeland against the expected American invasion. Their situation was far worse than they knew. In secret, the

Soviets had promised Roosevelt that they would enter the war against Japan in August 1945. And by July 1945 the first atomic bomb had been tested and the second was ready for use.

Research directed toward producing the atomic bomb had begun in earnest four years before, and by 1945 some $2 billion had been spent and some 150,000 people were at work on the project. By April 1945, the scientists were confident that the bomb would function, and President Truman established an interim committee to advise him regarding the use of atomic weapons. The eight-man interim committee was advised by a four-man scientific panel, including Enrico Fermi and J. Robert Oppenheimer.

The scientists on the project had mixed feelings as to how the bomb should be used. Many had joined the project out of fear that Nazi Germany would develop an atomic bomb before the Allies did. Now that Germany had been defeated, their principal motive for developing the weapon was gone. Some felt that the bomb should not be used at all. A greater number, represented in a document called The Franck Report, suggested that the initial bomb be dropped on an unpopulated demonstration area, leaving military use for later, should the Japanese fail to surrender. Many others felt that the atomic bomb should be used like any other bomb. By May 1945 this meant that it should be dropped dead center on a Japanese city.

On 1 June, the interim committee met and voted for a military use of the bomb, without warning, at the earliest possible moment. On 16 June, the scientific panel concurred: "We can propose no technical demonstration likely to bring an end to the war." Truman had no difficulty agreeing, and the bomb fell on Hiroshima at 8:15 A.M. on 6 August 1945. An eleven-year-old in Hiroshima wrote:

> From outside the front entrance an indescribable color and light came thrusting in. . . . Everything in sight which could be called a building was crushed to the ground and sending out flames. . . . At the side of Kyobashi river burned people were moaning, "Hot" "Hot" and jumping into the river. . . . The river became not a stream of flowing water but a stream of drifting dead bodies. No matter how much I might exaggerate the stories of burned people . . . the facts were more terrible; on this point I ask for pardon. (Akira Osada, *Children of the A-Bomb*, p. 219)

Estimates of the dead at Hiroshima range from 80,000 to 120,000 people. Three days later, an atomic bomb exploded over Nagasaki, killing about 50,000 people and wounding 50,000 more.

The main moral argument for the use of an atomic bomb on Hiroshima, developed by Secretary of War Stimson in an article in 1947, was that dropping the bomb saved lives on balance. If the bomb had not been dropped, incendiary raids on Japanese cities would have continued, and Hiroshima and Nagasaki would have been destroyed anyway. If the bomb had not been dropped, a naval blockade would have been thrown around Japan, causing mass starvation. If the bomb had not been dropped, a land invasion by the Americans would have caused many more casualties, on both sides, than the casualties at Hiroshima and Nagasaki. The atomic bomb was special, Stimson wrote, and it administered a "special shock" to Japan that produced surrender without more air raids, without a blockade, and without a land invasion.

The scientists who wrote The Franck Report did not contest that as many people could be killed with conventional weapons as with atomic bombs. But they argued that use of the atomic bomb would have special negative repercussions in the postwar period. Use of an atomic weapon in war would make other nations clamor to have it as well, producing an atomic arms race that might have disastrous consequences for mankind. According to the scientists, a refusal to use the device would make international control of atomic weapons—the only alternative to an atomic arms race—more feasible. Though Truman and Stimson did not rebut this argument, they might have argued that an exhibition in war of the awfulness of atomic weapons might make the case for internationalization more compelling. The use of poison gas in World War I helped rather than hindered the movement to ban poison gas after the war was over.

Nevertheless, many people think that bombing Hiroshima was immoral, that it disgraced the United States and forever tarnished the glory of a just victory in the Pacific, won at great cost by American soldiers, sailors, airmen, and marines. Most vividly, the attack was a direct attack on Japanese civilians, including many small children, in violation of the principle of discrimination. Truman tried to hide this in his announcement that the first atomic bomb had fallen "on Hiroshima, a military base" (*The Truman Administration*, p. 39), but such prevarication is one way of admitting guilt. Perhaps more people died in the Tokyo incendiary raid than at Hiroshima. But all of the fire raids were direct attacks on Japanese civilians, designed to "break the Japanese will to resist," and all of the fire raids were therefore indiscriminate. The earlier raid on Tokyo established no moral precedent that might be cited to justify Hiroshima.

LeMay's predecessor, Heywood Hansel, believed this, and his resistance to firebombing cost him his job. But for people like LeMay and Stimson, the distinction between civilian and soldier was not morally relevant. "The face of war is the face of death," Stimson wrote, implying that it does not much matter whose death it is. For Stimson, what matters morally is choosing the option that produces victory while taking the smallest number of lives. In that light, what were Stimson's and Truman's options in early August 1945?

The choice for the United States in August 1945 was *not*, as Stimson and many others have alleged, between dropping the atomic bomb and invading Japan, since the land invasion of Japan was not scheduled to begin until November. Nor was there a forced choice between atomic raids and further incendiary raids, since most of Japan's cities had already been destroyed, and the military significance of destroying one or two more with incendiary bombs was negligible. Nor was there a choice between using atomic weapons and starving the population, since the Japanese had sufficient food to endure a blockade of many months. The real choices *in August 1945* were (a) don't use the bomb and seek a negotiated peace, (b) demonstrate the bomb and seek a negotiated peace, and (c) use the bomb on a city and hope for unconditional surrender.

The "unconditional surrender" of Japan was the announced goal of the American war effort. But in fact there is no such thing as unconditional surrender, since each side in a war has objectives that constitute their conditions of peace. The American goals in the Pacific theater, announced at Cairo, called for the return or liberation of Japanese-occupied territories, Japanese disarmament, and a temporary occupation of Japan. Though these terms had been rejected, by January 1945 the Japanese leadership knew that military defeat was inevitable. They sought to explore terms of surrender through the Russians from February on, and a new premier was appointed in April, carrying the hopes of the emperor for an early negotiated peace. Joseph Grew, the former American ambassador to Japan, suggested to Roosevelt that the Japanese were prepared to surrender on the sole condition that the dignity of the emperor be preserved. But Truman's Potsdam declaration on 26 July gave no assurances concerning the emperor at a time when many American newspapers, sensing victory, were demanding that Emperor Hirohito be tried as a war criminal. The Potsdam terms were rejected by Japan, and Truman, with the bomb in his pocket, was in no mood to negotiate.

Given the Japanese attacks on Pearl Harbor, the United States had just cause for war with Japan. Would this just cause have been lost if the position of the emperor was guaranteed before surrender? The Potsdam declaration insisted on unconditional surrender. But less than one month later, on 11 August, the American secretary of state assured the Japanese in writing that they could keep their emperor, and the Japanese agreed to surrender *on this condition* three days afterward. Certainly what was morally right in August 1945 must also have been morally right in July. So there is a strong possibility that a morally acceptable change in the Potsdam declaration could have induced surrender in July, and that would have saved the most lives of all.

Given American inflexibility regarding terms, what contribution did the atomic attacks make toward inducing the surrender of 14 August? Critics of Hiroshima and Nagasaki argue that the attacks were neither necessary nor sufficient to end the war. They were not necessary, because Japan was already thoroughly defeated and, as the American Strategic Bombing Survey concluded, would have surrendered even if the atomic bombs were never used. They were not sufficient, because, as it turned out, the same three (of six) top Japanese leaders who opposed surrender before Hiroshima and Nagasaki still opposed surrender after the atomic attacks.

Defenders of the atomic bombings will argue that the use of a new weapon gave the emperor the trump card that broke the three-three deadlock in the Imperial Conference. But if "something new" was needed, a demonstration bombing outside a city might have served as well.

What, then, explains Truman's intransigence at Potsdam and his eagerness to use the bomb? For the intransigence, consider the anger and hatred the American people felt toward Japan, and Truman's desire to get no less from Japan than Churchill and Stalin had gotten from Germany. For the eagerness, consider the fact that the bomb had always been intended for use "as soon as possible," that Truman believed that it would produce surrender on his own terms, and that, with the Soviets entering the war on 8 August, delay in obtaining surrender would force the Americans to share victory laurels with the Soviets, a discomfiting thought all around. But none of these political and psychological reasons produce a *moral* rationale for the attack on Hiroshima. If the facts are as given here, the attack was probably not necessary, probably not proportionate, and certainly not discriminate.

5. REVOLUTIONARY WAR AND COUNTERINSURGENCY TACTICS

In the immediate aftermath of Hiroshima, many felt that war would abolish man or that man would abolish war. The good news after 1945 was that war did not abolish man. The bad news was that there was no end to war. The many wars that followed World War II were often wars in a different style, not the familiar wars of state against state but wars in which "substate" revolutionary or secessionist movements pitted themselves against established state power. In some cases, as in China, Cuba, and Nicaragua, the principal goal of the revolutionaries was a radical change in the existing social system. Elsewhere, as in Vietnam, Algeria, and Angola, the principal goal of the revolutionaries was the expulsion of foreign power. In still other cases, as in Pakistan, Nigeria, and Ethiopia, secessionists sought to carve a new state out of some fraction of an existing nation. In all these countries, the sort of war that transpired only occasionally took the traditional European form of pitched battles between massed formations. The ambush, the raid, sabotage, and other guerrilla tactics became the normal modes of war. In these conflicts, military forces, guerrillas, and counterinsurgents alike split their efforts between military activities and political work.

Revolutionary war poses difficult problems for the moral critic. The traditional *jus in bello*, developed in the context of European interstate war, is often inapplicable to revolutionary struggles. For the revolutionaries, many of the traditional rules of war, "carrying arms openly" and "having a fixed distinctive sign recognizable at a distance," for example, are invitations to suicide and unilaterally helpful to regimes in power. For the counterinsurgents, the distinction between soldier and civilian, so emphasized in the modern *jus in bello*, seems undercut by the circumstances of "people's war," in which the revolutionaries are hidden among the civilian population, which supports them, as Mao Tse-tung wrote, like water supports the fish in the sea.

Not all complaints about the irrelevance of traditional rules of war to revolutionary struggles are justified. Many of the rules of war set out in the Hague and Geneva Conventions can be followed by both revolutionaries and counterinsurgents, and followed without significant prejudice to their chances of victory. The "forbidden means of injury" given in the Hague Convention of 1907: the use of poison or poisoned weapons, killing or wounding after betraying promises of safety, killing or wounding persons who have surrendered, declarations of no quarter, using weapons or projectiles that cause undue damage or suffering, abusing the Red Cross, looting, pillage, and other unnecessary destruction, are such that it is difficult to imagine either side gaining substantially by ignoring them. All these rules can and should apply to revolutionary war. Only in the cases in which one side senses an advantage in violating the laws of war does moral restraint face a real challenge in revolutionary wars. Two tactics that fall into this category are torture of prisoners and assassination.

(a) Torture

The Third Geneva Convention expressly forbids the torture of prisoners of war. Because the use of torture is universally despised, no regime or movement will publicly acknowledge its use. Nevertheless, the use of torture is common in counterrevolutionary warfare, especially for the extraction of information, since revolutionary activists do not identify themselves and the regime in power has a vital stake in determining who its enemies are. (The revolutionaries have no corresponding difficulty identifying the officials and troops of the regime in power.) Commanders of counterinsurgency forces often presume that torture will provide vital information that cannot be obtained in any other way.

But the presumption that torture will produce information that cannot be obtained in any other way is true for all wars, not just revolutionary wars. Prisoners of war in World War II often possessed important military information that their captors could not obtain without the use of torture. Nevertheless, not even Hitler felt that these circumstances justified the torture of prisoners of war. Torture may be "necessary," but not all necessary acts are justifiable acts, in traditional war or any other kind of war.

Governments notorious for the torture of revolutionaries—the French in Algeria, the Saigon regime, the Pahlavi government in Iran— argue that captured revolutionary guerrillas are not prisoners of war, but common criminals not entitled to the protection of the laws of war. But the "proofs" that revolutionary guerrillas are not soldiers but criminals usually point to circumstances, like the absence of uniforms and the use of ambushes, that in fact are legal according to the law of war. The real excuse for torture is military convenience, combined with intense feelings that suppressing the revolution is a great moral cause.

In developing arguments against the use of torture, we should not make the parallel error of appealing to the justice of revolutionary goals. Some revolutionary causes—the Falangist cause in Spain in 1936, for example—have been manifestly unjust. Nor does the fact that torture causes suffering suffice to condemn the practice, since war causes immense suffering of all kinds. The principal moral argument against torture is that the practice of torture requires morally twisted characters, persons who are hardly likely to confine their activities to the strict limits of military need. Once the practice is established, torture is invariably used for revenge, for intimidation, and for other purposes unrelated to the extraction of information. In these cases the pretense of military necessity is absurd.

Furthermore, the argument that torture is a military necessity is based on mistaken assumptions about the usefulness of torture. So far from being militarily necessary, experience shows that the practice is in fact useless and self-defeating. It is useless because information obtained under torture is notoriously unreliable. It is self-defeating because the practice of torture by a government is the surest way to destroy popular support for counter-revolutionary war. Thus, for the French, for the South Vietnamese, and for the Shah, the use of torture played into the hands of the revolutionaries.

(b) Assassination

In the law of war, political officials are traditionally treated as non-combatants. As such, they are not legitimate targets for military violence, and the killing of political officials counts not as war but murder. But in many revolutions, the head of state opposed by the revolutionaries is also the head of the national army, and in such cases, assassination might be seen as a certifiable act of war. It follows from this that captured revolutionaries acting as assassins may be entitled to treatment as prisoners of war. But it does not follow from this that such acts of war are morally legitimate acts.

(c) The Vietcong Assassination Campaign

In 1961 alone, the Vietcong (the Saigon name for the NLF) in South Vietnam killed over 4,000 village chiefs, policemen, and other officials of the Saigon regime. Putting questions of international law aside, what can be said about the moral legitimacy of this Vietcong campaign?

One could stand one's ground and argue that such killings are immoral because they disregard the principle of noncombatant immunity. But before we do this, we should ask again what the moral grounds for the principle of noncombatant immunity are. Part of these grounds involves the idea that civilians, as such, simply live their lives, and do not seek to impose political ends. Consequently, if one is waging war, that is, using violence for a political purpose, civilians should not be one's targets, since they do not block the way to political goals. On the other hand, those officials of the government who are involved primarily in exercising political control—Saigon-appointed village chiefs, for example, and not technicians in the department of agriculture—seem to be appropriate targets for revolutionary violence. Such government officials choose their line of work, and if they choose this work in a period of revolutionary agitation, they know that their work has risks. (The Vietcong, in fact, often issued preliminary warnings to local Saigon officials to resign their jobs "or else".) For these reasons, it seems a mistake to put South Vietnamese government officials into the protected moral class of "innocent noncombatants."

Despite this argument, it is difficult to sympathize with Vietcong assassination tactics. The purpose of the assassinations was to demonstrate the lack of control Diem exercised over the countryside and to provoke Diem into repressive measures that would serve to increase the popularity of the revolutionary cause. In both respects the campaign was successful, and Diem became so unpopular that the Vietcong came to regret that he was deposed before their control of South Vietnam was complete. But though the assassination campaign achieved short-run objectives, it did not serve the long-term Vietcong goals: the expulsion of the Americans and the achievement of social revolution in South Vietnam. The controlling factor in South Vietnam in the early 1960s was the South Vietnamese Army, which the Vietcong had either to defeat or to subvert. There is little direct connection between assassinating village chiefs and winning over the Army, and one suspects that the brutality exhibited in the assassination campaign won as many hearts for Saigon as it did for the Vietcong.

When Diem fell in 1963, the Army remained loyal to Saigon, and the revolutionaries obtained for their constituents only more dictatorship and American intervention on a massive scale. When Saigon surrendered in 1975, assassination was a discarded tactic. The science of winning revolutions is even less developed than the science of winning battles, and arguments that assassination is necessary or sufficient for successful revolution are correspondingly weak. Those who believe that all violence, including revolutionary violence, requires a moral justification may judge that assassination of political officials in South Vietnam violated necessity and proportionality, even if those officials did not deserve the protection of noncombatant immunity.

6. COUNTERINSURGENCY AND COMMAND
RESPONSIBILITY: THE MASSACRE AT MY LAI

On 7:24 A.M., 16 March 1968, workers in the fields around the hamlet of
My Lai, in the northern part of South Vietnam, suddenly found themselves
under artillery attack. The workers jumped into the rice paddies and buffalo wallows; people in nearby settlements rushed to primitive shelters built
under their homes. Two American Shark helicopter gunships flew over the
village, firing machine guns and rockets toward the western side of the
hamlet. More American helicopters appeared and landed, and a company
of American soldiers under Capt. Ernest Medina jumped off, firing their
M-16s to secure the landing area. Overhead, in helicopters, Col. Oran
Henderson and Maj. Gen. Samuel Koster observed the operation, the
largest that day in Quang Ngai province, an area generally favorable to the
Vietcong.

At 7:50, two platoons of soldiers moved east through My Lai. The
first platoon, consisting of two squads of about 25 men commanded by Lt.
William Calley, moved through the subhamlet of My Lai 4, shooting some
Vietnamese as they ran, bayoneting others, throwing hand grenades into
huts, shooting livestock, and destroying crops. The first squad, under Sgt.
David Mitchell, proceeded further, rounding up two groups of Vietnamese
women, children, and old men (the younger men being in the paddies,
away fighting, or killed in the war). One group of 20 to 50 people was shot
south of the hamlet. Another, larger group of perhaps 150 people was put
in a ditch on the south side of My Lai 4. Lt. Calley reached the ditch at 9:00.
At 9:15 Calley and members of the first platoon began firing at the ditch,
and kept on firing until everyone in the ditch seemed shot to pieces. A few
children, shielded by their mothers' bodies, survived. When one small child
crawled out, the soldiers shot him and threw him back in the ditch.

Meanwhile the second platoon, consisting of three squads under Lt.
Steven K. Brooks, was moving through the north side of My Lai 4. As they
advanced, they shot civilians fleeing toward the rice paddies. They threw
hand grenades into the huts, and shot down anyone who tried to emerge.
By 8:30, at least 100 civilians had been killed on the north side, and at least
2 Vietnamese women had been raped. At 8:45, the second platoon
rounded up 10 to 20 women, forced them to sit in a circle, and fired hand
grenades into their midst. Those who escaped the grenades were shot
down by automatic weapons fire.

At 9:15 Medina told the second platoon, "That's enough for today."
But the first platoon and the third platoon, newly flown in, continued
killing for another hour, shooting a number of wounded Vietnamese lying
on the ground. At 1:30 P.M. the three platoons left the hamlet, moving
east. Not a single shot had been fired at the Americans since they landed at
My Lai. Captain Medina reported to his superiors that 90 Vietcong had
been killed in action. In the village, perhaps 400 people were dead. There

was one American casualty. Private Carter of the first platoon had shot himself in the foot, rather than go on with this kind of war.

The incidents described here are not disputed by the U.S. government. They were substantiated in courts-martial conducted by the Army, by a special subcommittee of the House Armed Services Committee, by a special inquiry initiated by the secretary of the army, by pictures of corpses taken by Army photographers, and by tapes of radio conversations between the men on the ground and the helicopters above. Nor is it disputed that the events at My Lai were terrible crimes, for which no moral or legal justification is possible. The problem is to determine who is responsible.

In judging complex events with many participants, one logical point about moral responsibility is critical. Many people believe that if one person is fully responsible for a crime, others cannot be responsible, as if guilt were an indivisible lump handed to one person or another. But moral guilt is indefinitely expandable, and if one person is completely responsible for a crime, others can be completely responsible too. We should not think that if the men at the bottom are responsible for My Lai, the men at the top are not, or that if the men at the top are responsible, the men at the bottom are not.

The logical starting point is at the bottom, with the men who did the shooting. As it happens, Lieutenant Calley did more shooting than anyone else, and he was one of the men court-martialed after the massacre. During his trial, polls showed that many Americans, perhaps a majority, felt that Calley's conduct was excusable.

At his trial and in his memoirs, Calley offered two defenses for his actions at My Lai. First, he claimed that he was acting under orders. Second, he argued that it was impossible to tell soldiers from civilians in Vietnam.

To this day, no one is sure what Medina's orders to Calley were. From reports, it seems that Medina told his men to engage the enemy, move them out of the hamlet, and destroy everything left behind. He also told them there would be no civilians in the village, which meant that every person in My Lai qualified as an enemy. By implication, then, Medina ordered Calley to attack everyone in the hamlet.

Calley took these orders to mean *kill* everyone in the hamlet. If children and babies were in the hamlet, the orders meant to kill them, too. Certainly it was possible to interpret Medina's orders in this way. But even if there was such an order, it was clearly illegal by international law, by conventions ratified by the United States, and by the [American] Uniform Code of Military Justice. The problem, then, is to determine when a soldier is obliged to refuse an illegal order.

In an earlier My Lai trial, the presiding judge instructed the court that the defendant, Sergeant Hutton, was obliged to disobey an order if he knew it was illegal or if it "was manifestly illegal on its face." In Calley's trial, the judge instructed that Calley was obliged to disobey orders if he knew they were unlawful or if they were such that "a man of ordinary sense and reasoning under the circumstances [would] know to be unlawful." By either standard, Calley was obliged to disobey the orders he thought he was given. The fact that he did not know this is no excuse. As the reviewing court noted, "Heed must be given not only to subjective innocence-through-ignorance in the soldier, but also to the consequences for his victims."

This leaves Calley's argument that one cannot identify the enemy in a guerrilla war. In some cases this is true, but it does not follow that it was true in this case. Generally, one *can* identify the enemy by his behavior if not by his uniform, and no one at My Lai offered resistance to the Americans. Furthermore, by all the laws of war, one must not kill the helpless wounded, those who surrender, or babies.

What about Calley's superiors, Captain Medina, Colonel Henderson, Major General Koster? The Army inquiry, conducted by General Peers, concluded that they failed to pursue accusations of war crimes and were actively involved in suppressing knowledge of the incident. Indeed, the Army would have taken no action whatsoever about My Lai had not several congressmen, tipped off by a private letter, decided to pursue the story.

Obviously, if it was wrong to kill the people of My Lai, it was wrong to cover up the killing. For ethics, the more serious issue is the question of the degree to which Medina, Henderson, Koster, and other higher-ups were responsible for the massacre itself.

Captain Medina, by issuing imprecise orders that showed no concern for the possibility of civilian casualties, and by failing to stop a massacre in progress, is fully implicated. Furthermore, American tactics at this point in the war—which made almost all Quang Ngai province a "free fire zone" open to unauthorized air attacks, which condoned thousands of assassinations of alleged Vietcong cadres in the CIA's Phoenix Operation, which made "search and destroy" operations the norm for Quang Ngai villages and defoliation with herbicides the norm for the fields—exhibited such a disregard for civilian life that My Lai was bound to happen sooner or later. At the end of World War II, the United States executed Gen. Tomoyuki Yamashita for atrocities committed by his soldiers in the Philippines—crimes that, in the chaos of imminent defeat, he did not know about and could not have prevented. It is an extreme measure to use such strict standards of liability for the top levels of military command, but, had the Yamashita standard been applied in Vietnam, it might have produced in the officers in charge the energy and concern that could have prevented My Lai and other tragedies like it.

William Calley was tried for "killing 109 Oriental human beings, whose names and sexes are unknown." He was convicted and sentenced to life in prison. The review court reduced his sentence to 20 years; the secretary of the army reduced it to 10. He served three years. No one else was convicted of anything.

7. TERRORISM AND COUNTERTERRORISM

As the last of the great colonial empires were dismantled in the 1970s, the attention of Europeans and Americans was increasingly diverted from the problem of revolution to the problem of terrorism. According to Vice-President Bush's Task Force on Combating Terrorism, terrorism is "the unlawful use or threat of violence against persons or property to further political or social objectives" (Report of the Vice-President's Task Force on Combating Terrorism, p. 1). By *that* definition of terrorism, George Washington was a terrorist. To distinguish terrorists from legitimate revolutionaries, a more restrictive definition is required.

What separates the terrorist from the traditional revolutionary is a persistent refusal to direct violence at military objectives. Terrorism, on this account, is the threat or use of violence against noncombatants for political purposes. In ordinary war, the deaths of civilians are side effects of military operations directed against military targets. In terrorist operations, the civilian is the direct and intentional target of attack. By this standard, George Washington was not a terrorist, nor was the truck-bomb attack on the Marine compound in Beirut in 1983 terrorism, though it was commonly described as such.

According to the traditional rule of discrimination, direct attacks against civilians are never morally justified. It follows from the rule of discrimination that terrorism is never morally justified, no matter how morally urgent the goals of the terrorists. But the rule of discrimination relies on a distinction between "foreseen but unintended deaths" and "direct and intended deaths" that some philosophers have found logically questionable. For philosophers who do not accept the rule of discrimination, it is the rule of proportionality that provides the crucial moral test of terrorism. Can terrorism serve a just cause in such a way that its good effects substantially outweigh the bad? The verdict of history is clear: almost never. Most terrorists do not support just causes. As for the few that do, their actions are almost invariably ineffective.

Terrorism comes in two varieties: state terrorism and substate terrorism. State terrorism involves the use of terrorism by governments for purposes of political intimidation. Substate terrorism involves the use of terrorism by political groups. Though state terrorism receives less publicity, it is generally larger in scale than substate terrorism. The portion of Allied bombing in World War II devoted to "breaking civilian morale," the imprisonment of dissidents in the Soviet Gulag, the widespread use of murder and torture to crush dissent in Brazil (after 1964), Indonesia (after

1965), Greece (after 1967), Uruguay (after 1973), Chile (after 1973), Argentina (after 1976), and Guatemala (after 1978) are instances of state terrorism that each claimed thousands or tens of thousands of lives. We have already analyzed the terrorism involved in Allied bombing in World War II, and have found little in moral theory to justify these direct attacks on German and Japanese civilians. All of the other cases of state terrorism listed here, not prompted by the supreme emergency of attacks by the Axis, rate even lower on the moral scale.

By the CIA's estimate, substate terrorist groups killed 3,668 civilians between 1968 and 1980, a small fraction of the toll reaped by state terrorism. Nevertheless, Western governments are intensely concerned with substate terrorism, because citizens of Western nations are much more likely to be victims of terrorist groups than of terrorist governments. When department stores are bombed, planes hijacked, and journalists kidnapped, the citizenry naturally demands that the government "do something" about terrorism. Military remedies are frequently proposed. The question is whether these remedies involve an appropriate and morally justifiable use of force.

(a) The Raid on Entebbe

Of all the military actions undertaken against terrorists since World War II none has been more celebrated than the Israeli raid on the airport at Entebbe, Uganda, in 1976. Soon the subject of several movies, the Entebbe raid was hailed by many as a model of successful antiterrorist action. From a military point of view, the raid was a brilliant success. But was it an equally brilliant success from the moral point of view?

The Entebbe story began on 27 June 1976, when four terrorists boarded an Air France Tel Aviv-to-Paris flight during its stopover at Athens. The terrorists—Wilfrid Böse, Gabriele Tidemann, and two Arab men—ordered the plane, with its 247 passengers and crew of 12, to fly south. The plane stopped at Benghazi, Libya, refueled, and landed the next morning at Entebbe, Uganda. The hijackers, joined by six more armed Arabs, moved the passengers and crew to the old terminal building, which was surrounded and guarded by Ugandan soldiers.

On 28 June, the hijackers announced that 53 designated prisoners— 40 in Israel, 6 in West Germany, 5 in Kenya, 1 in France, and 1 in Switzerland—must be released from jail by 30 June, or the plane and its passengers would be blown up. The list of the designated prisoners is worth studying. It included three persons held in Germany for the kidnapping of businessman Peter Lorenz and the murder of a German judge; Kozo Okamoto, convicted of murder in Israel for participating in the massacre of 24 civilians at Lod Airport; and William Nasser, convicted of murder in Israel in 1968. But it also included, among the Israeli prisoners, Archbishop Hilarion Carpucci, convicted of gunrunning; Muzna Nicola, held for espionage; Samir Darwish, jailed for planning an escape of Arab detainees from Ramleh Prison; and 36 other Arabs held on a variety of lesser charges. The government of Israel, citing its policy of nonnegotiation with terrorists, rejected the demands point-blank. The responses of other governments holding designated prisoners were slightly more ambiguous, but uniformly negative.

On 29 June the hostages were visited by Ugandan President Idi Amin, who announced that the next move was up to the government of Israel. At 7:00 that evening, the terrorists isolated all hostages holding Israeli passports in a separate room. After several fruitless appeals to Amin to exert pressure on the terrorists, the Israeli government announced on 1 July that it was "prepared to begin negotiations . . . for the liberation of the prisoners in exchange for a certain number of prisoners in Israel." According to reports, this news was almost uniformly received with joy by the hostages. The same day, the hijackers released 47 hostages; the next day, they released 101 more. All who remained, except for the Air France crew, were Israeli citizens.

While the Israeli government began discussions with the terrorists, Defense Minister Shimon Peres developed plans for a rescue attempt, Project Thunderbolt. The plans took shape on 2 July and received cabinet approval on 3 July. Four Hercules C-130 transport aircraft flew from Israel down the Red Sea and across Ethiopia and Kenya, landing at the end of the runway at Entebbe around 11 P.M. A black Mercedes, resembling Idi Amin's, rolled off a C-130 and up to the guard post at the control tower. The confused Ugandans saluted and were shot by Israelis from inside the car. Seconds later, Israeli commandos burst into the terminal building, shooting Bose and Tidemann immediately and ordering the hostages (in Hebrew) to fall on the floor. Two minutes later, seven terrorists and two hostages were dead, at least one of them killed accidentally by Israeli bullets.

While the hostages were loaded on the first C-130, commandos from the other two planes engaged Ugandan forces at different locations in the airport, and the team from the fourth plane set about blowing up MIG 231 fighters belonging to the Ugandan Air Force. In less than an hour, all four planes were aloft and on their way to Nairobi, Kenya, to refuel. Two Israeli soldiers and 20 to 50 Ugandan troops lay dead. Of the 107 Israeli hostages, the commandos had brought 103 home alive. Two hostages had died at Entebbe, and one died of wounds on the flight back. The last hostage, Mrs. Dora Black, had been removed to a hospital in Kampala, near Entebbe, on 2 July. After 4 July, she was never seen again.

If there are just uses of force, the killing of Bose, Tidemann, and other terrorists in the Entebbe incident was morally legitimate. The problem of whether the raid as a whole was morally legitimate centers on the questions of whether the commandos violated the rights of Ugandans and the rights of the hostages.

In the United Nations debate in the days following the raid, the Israeli ambassador, Chaim Herzog, argued on the basis of circumstantial evidence that Idi Amin had conspired with the terrorists before the raid took place. Amin's hatred of Jews, his admiration of Hitler, his support for the Palestinian cause, and the murderous brutality of his government in Uganda were well known. Furthermore, there was some evidence that the airport at Entebbe was prepared to receive a group of prisoners, and throughout the incident the Ugandan soldiers and Amin seemed on friendly terms with the terrorists. Nevertheless, the evidence cited by Herzog—that Bose is reported to have said "We are safe" on landing at Entebbe, that the terrorist reinforcements arrived at Entebbe in a black Mercedes, and so forth—was hardly such as would prove conspiracy in a court of law; and the conduct of the Ugandan government in handling the situation was scarcely different from what any government would have contrived under the circumstances.

If the hijackers, for example, had flown to New York, it is likely that the American authorities would have guarded the airport, would have supplied food and water, would not have attempted a rescue on their own, and would have resisted an armed assault on Kennedy Airport by unknown persons in the middle of the night. Even if the murderous character of the Amin regime makes it painful to speak of the rights of the Ugandan government and state in this matter, according to international law the raid constituted an illegal attack by Israel against Uganda. Unless one is convinced of a prior plan between Bose and Amin, one must feel sympathy for the Ugandan soldiers who died in the attack. They were, by and large, simply doing their jobs, and the Israelis, by their own admission, shot at them first.

At first sight, it seems odd to wonder whether Project Thunderbolt violated the rights of the hostages it was designed to rescue. But the rescue attempt put the lives of the hostages at risk, and the question must be faced of whether the risk was too great. In May 1974, when Israeli commandos stormed a school at Maalot (in northern Israel) in which 100 children were held by terrorists, 22 children were killed in the cross fire before the rescue was completed. Considering the greater physical obstacles confronting a rescue at Entebbe, the Israeli government reckoned on 30 dead and 50 wounded among the hostages and its own forces, and it was safe to assume that at least that many casualties might be suffered on the Ugandan side. Is it morally permissible to initiate a course of action that will get 60 people killed in order to save 100 people? As it happened, things turned out much better than expected, but the decision of 3 July had to be made, and must be evaluated, on the basis of the best estimates of casualties available to the Israeli government at the time.

Suppose that, on the best evidence available, the prediction was that 20 hostages would be killed in the rescue, and suppose that you were one of the hostages. If asked by your government, would you have freely consented to the rescue attempt, thereby accepting a 19 percent chance of death? Or would you have preferred that your government continue to negotiate with the terrorists, in hopes of obtaining a less immediate but less dangerous release? For those hostages who would *not* have freely consented to this style of rescue if they had been asked, the raid on Entebbe was morally in violation of their rights.

If we accept this argument and conclude that the Entebbe raid violated the rights of some Israeli hostages and Ugandan soldiers, and the sovereignty of Uganda, it does not follow automatically that the raid was morally mistaken. Every other alternative might have been morally worse. Let us consider the unpalatable but feasible alternative of simply giving in. Imagine that the 40 designated prisoners in Israel were assembled, brought to Uganda, and exchanged for 107 Israeli hostages. The damage that such acquiescence would cause would include (a) the failure to punish justly imprisoned murderers like Okamoto; (b) failure to bring the hijackers to justice; (c) the possibility or probability of further criminal acts committed by released prisoners; (d) encouragement of world terrorism, producing an increased frequency of terrorist acts in the future. These are very serious results, but it is not clear that avoiding them justified a course of action that would surely produce some deaths right away. As it happened, terrorist groups did not seem particularly discouraged by the results at Entebbe, since there were plenty of terrorist hijackings in the years that followed.

As for the raid itself, it could be considered a complete moral success only if *all* the hostages came home safe, and only if some of the hostages would surely have died if the raid had not taken place. Since four hostages died who might have been saved, the raid was not a complete success, despite good fortune beyond the wildest dreams of those who planned it. It is interesting to compare the results at Entebbe with the results obtained by President Carter in the Iran hostage crisis of 1979–1981. By preference and by necessity, President Carter was forced to concede to terrorists, and the inglorious resolution of that crisis has been disparagingly compared with the Israeli success at Entebbe. But in the end, all of the hostages imprisoned in the American embassy in Tehran came home.

(b) The 1986 Attack on Libya

The 1980s saw the development of a novel form of terrorism: state sponsorship of substate terrorist groups. For many persons outside the United States, the most conspicuous example of such sponsorship was American support for quasi-military "contra" groups attempting to unseat the Sandinista government in Nicaragua. But for most Americans and for the American government, the prime example was the Qaddafi regime in Libya, which had in varying degrees financed, supplied, and assisted in training terrorist groups opposed to the government of Israel and its allies.

Relations between the United States and Libya following the military coup that brought Qaddafi to power in 1969 had never been been particularly good, but they deteriorated rapidly after President Reagan's election in 1980. Accusing the Qaddafi regime of supporting international terrorism, the United States closed the Libyan embassy in Washington in May 1981, and in August 1981 Navy F-14s shot down two Libyan fighter planes above the Gulf of Sidra.

In 1985, civilians around the world were subjected to an abnormally high number of terrorist attacks. In June, a TWA jetliner was hijacked to Beirut and an American serviceman was shot on the plane. In October, an Italian cruise ship was hijacked and an American tourist killed. In November, terrorists hijacked an Egyptian Boeing 737 to Malta, and 59 passengers were killed in a bungled rescue attempt. In December, terrorists attacked El-Al ticket counters at airports in Rome and Vienna, leaving 19 dead.

President Reagan accused Libya of supporting the terrorists involved in the Rome and Vienna attacks, and froze Libyan assets in American banks. In the succeeding months, American naval vessels holding exercises in the Gulf of Sidra, which Libya claims as territorial waters, were fired upon, and sank two Libyan patrol boats in return.

On 5 April 1986, a bomb went off in a Berlin discotheque, killing 2 and wounding 155, including about 60 Americans, 1 of whom died. Nine days later, 18 F-111 American fighter bombers and 15 A-6 Navy warplanes attacked Libya, bombing targets in Benghazi and Tripoli. According to Libyan sources, 16 were wounded and 15 died in these attacks, among them the adopted daughter of Colonel Qaddafi.

The next day, citing "irrefutable evidence" of Libyan involvement in the Berlin bombing, President Reagan characterized the raid as punitive retaliation for the Berlin attack. Secretary of Defense Weinberger and Secretary of State Shultz, rebutting charges that the raid was "terrorism in reverse," argued that American planes were specifically instructed to avoid civilian targets, and were directed to drop bombs only on military positions and terrorist training camps. In the months following, administration officials described the raid as a major success, noting that the bombing had chastened Qaddafi and other terrorists into uncharacteristic silence. In the five months before the raid, there had been 22 terrorist incidents claiming over 500 casualties. In the 4 months following the raid, there were 8 terrorist incidents claiming 22 casualties.

Critics of the raid will be quick to point out that a decline in terrorist incidents after the raid is no proof that the raid *caused* the decline. To some degree, the decline in casualties after the raid was a matter of luck. One month *after* the raid, security police at Heathrow Airport in London discovered a bomb on an Israeli jumbo jet just minutes before takeoff. Had the bomb exploded, the death toll would have been far greater than the toll for all terrorist incidents in 1985 combined. Obviously, this tragedy was averted by chance, not because the United States had bombed Libya. Furthermore, there were some terrorist acts that would not have been performed if the raid had not occurred. Four hostages of terrorists in Lebanon, one American and three Britons, were killed in late April in specific retaliation for the American raid and for British complicity with the Americans.

Furthermore, questions have been raised concerning American intentions in the raid. The announced intention was a specific reprisal against Qaddafi for the attack in Berlin. But on some accounts, the evidence linking Qaddafi to the Berlin attack was weak: West German security forces have never accepted it, and the information, consisting of intercepted Libyan cables in Arabic code, was never submitted to expert American interpreters for analysis. Finally, according to the American journalist Seymour Hersh, the target assigned to American F-111s was Qaddafi's tent, in which his immediate family lived. Even if we concede that Qaddafi, being a colonel, qualifies as a military target, his children do not qualify; and no one could say that the United States aimed at Qaddafi's residence without intending to kill the children who lived there. If the evidence bears out Hersh's charge that Qaddafi's residence was the primary target in the raid, the American attack, directed at civilians for political purposes, must be considered an act of terrorism.

8. SUGGESTIONS FOR FURTHER READING

Introduction

Two excellent introductions to the "laws of war" and their history are Sidney Bailey, *Prohibitions and Restraints in War* (New York: Oxford University Press, 1972); and Geoffrey Best, *Humanity in Warfare* (New York: Columbia University Press, 1972). See also *Restraints on War*, ed. Michael Howard (Oxford: Oxford University Press, 1979).

Necessity, Proportionality, and Discrimination

For the rule of necessity, see Paul Weiden, "Necessity in International Law," *Transactions of the Grotius Society* 24 (1939); N. C. H. Dunbar, "Military Necessity in War Crimes Trials," *British Year Book of International Law* 29 (1952); and William O'Brien, "The Meaning of 'Military Necessity' in International Law," *World Polity* 1 (1957).

The rule of proportionality is often discussed in connection with the legitimacy of a particular military reprisal. See Nicholas Greenwood Onuf, *Reprisals: Rituals, Rules, Rationales*, Research Monograph 42 (Princeton, NJ: Center for International Studies, Woodrow Wilson School of Public and International Affairs, 1974).

On noncombatant immunity, see Lester Nurick, "The Distinction

Between Combatants and Noncombatants in the Law of War," *American Journal of International Law* 39 (1945): 680–697; and Shelly Hartigan, *The Forgotten Victim: A History of the Civilian* (Chicago: Precedent Publishing, 1982). The controlling text for discussing the war rights of civilians is the Fourth Geneva Convention of 1949, "Convention Relative to the Protection of Civilian Persons in Times of War," reprinted in Leon Friedman, *The Laws of War: A Documentary History* (New York: Random House, 1972). For the philosophical complexities contained in the idea of noncombatant immunity, see Robert K. Fullinwider, "War and Innocence," *Philosophy and Public Affairs* (Fall 1975); and Lawrence A. Alexander, "Self-Defense and the Killing of Noncombatants," *Philosophy and Public Affairs* (Summer 1976).

The Need for a Theory of Jus in Bello

For a skeptical look at the laws of war that demonstrates a need for new moral foundations, see Donald A. Wells, *War Crimes and the Laws of War* (Lanham, MD: University Press of America, 1984).

Are the Laws of War Mere Conventions?

The classic defense of this view is George Mavrodes "Conventions and the Morality of War," *Philosophy and Public Affairs* (Winter 1975).

The Laws of War Promises

The noncontractual character of the laws of war was presumed at the Nuremberg trials at the end of World War II. The presumption was controversial at the time but is now generally accepted.

The Laws of War and Utilitarianism

One important utilitarian analysis of the laws of war is Richard Brandt, "Utilitarianism and the Laws of War," *Philosophy and Public Affairs* 1, no. 2 (Winter 1972).

The utilitarianism in this section is the traditional utilitarianism in which a single agent attempts to maximize the good in circumstances (including the choices of other agents) that are assumed to be fixed. Perhaps a stronger utilitarian analysis of the laws of war could be provided through the modern quasi-utilitarian system in which this assumption is dropped. See Donald Regan, *Utilitarianism and Co-operation* (Oxford: Oxford University Press, 1982); and David Gauthier, *Morals by Agreement* (Oxford: Clarendon Press, 1986).

Noncombatant Immunity and Chivalry

The laws of war in the age of chivalry are described in Maurice H. Keen, *The Laws of War in the Late Middle Ages* (Toronto: University of Toronto Press, 1965).

Direct and Indirect Killing

The distinction between direct and indirect killing seems to have been first developed by Jeremy Bentham in *Principles of Morals and of Legislation* Ch. VIII (1793). For further readings see the notes for Ch. 2, Sec. "Antiwar Pacificism."

The Case of Strategic Bombing

A good compact history of strategic bombing is Lee Kennett, *A History of Strategic Bombing* (New York: Scribner's, 1982).

Various works of Giulio Douhet were translated by Dino Ferrari and published together as *Command of the Air* (New York: Coward-McCann, 1942).The Hague Conventions for Air Warfare are printed in Leon Friedman, *The Laws of War.*

Of J. M. Spaight's many books on air power in the interwar period, the two most important are *Air Power and War Rights* (London: Longmans, Green, 1924) and *Air Power and the Cities* (London: Longmans, Green, 1930).

The Bomber Offensive Against Germany

The official history of the British bomber offensive is Sir Charles Webster and Noble Frankland, *The Strategic Air Offensive Against Germany*, 4 vols. (London: Her Majesty's Stationery Office, 1961); a good one-volume history is Max Hastings, *Bomber Command* (New York: Dial, 1979). A dizzyingly detailed account of shifts in British bombing policy is given in Anthony Verrier, *The Bomber Offensive* (New York: Macmillan, 1968).

Justification of the bombing campaign from 1942 on, by the man who led it, is presented in Arthur Harris, *Bomber Offensive* (London: Collings, 1947). Further pro-bombing justification is given in J. M. Spaight, *Bombing Vindicated* (London: Geoffrey Bles, 1944).

For criticism of the bombing campaign see F. J. P. Veale, *Advance to Barbarism* (London: Thompson and Smith, 1948); Sir Gerald Dickens, *Bombing and Strategy: The Fallacy of Total War* (London: Sampson Low, Marston, 1949); and Hans Rumpf, *The Bombing of Germany* (London: White Lion, 1963). For what it was like on the receiving end, see Hastings, *Bomber Command*, Ch. 13; Alexander McKee, *Dresden: The Devil's Tinderbox* (New York: Dutton, 1982); Martin Middlebrook, *The Battle of Hamburg* (New

York: Scribner's, 1981); and Kurt Vonnegut, *Slaughterhouse Five* (New York: Delacorte, 1969).

The entire speech of Bishop Bell is reprinted in George Bell, *The Church and Humanity* (London: Longmans, 1946).

American Bombing and Hiroshima

The official history of the American bombing campaign is Wesley Frank Craven and James Lea Cate, *The Army Air Forces in World War II*, 7 vols. (Chicago: University of Chicago Press, 1948–1958). The Army Air Force postwar assessment of strategic bombing has been edited by David MacIssac and reissued as *The United States Strategic Bombing Survey*, 10 vols. (New York: Garland, 1976).

For the development of American bombing policy in Europe, see Thomas M. Coffey, *Decision over Schweinfurt: The U.S. 8th Air Force Battle for Daylight Bombing* (New York: David MacKay, 1977). The development of bombing policy in the Pacific is summarized in Kennett, *History of Strategic Bombing*. The bombing of Japan is described from bombing crews' standpoint in Wilbur H. Morrison, *Point of No Return* (New York: Times Books, 1979); and from the standpoint of the people on the ground in Martin Caidin, *A Torch to the Enemy: The Fire Raid on Tokyo* (New York: Ballantine Books, 1960). The most thorough and eloquent account of American bombing policy is Michael Sherry, *The Rise of American Air Power* (New Haven: Yale University Press, 1987.)

The scientific steps leading to the A-bomb are described in Ronald Clark, *The Greatest Power on Earth* (New York: Harper and Row, 1980). The history of the decision to drop the bomb is described in the semiofficial *History of the Atomic Energy Commission, Vol I: The New World*, by Richard Hewlitt and Oscar Anderson (University Park: State University of Pennsylvania Press, 1962); and more critically in Gregg Herken, *The Winning Weapon* (New York: Knopf, 1980). The opposition of Leo Szilard and other atomic scientists to use of the bomb against a city is chronicled in Alice Kimball Smith, *A Peril and a Hope* (Chicago: University of Chicago Press, 1965).

For the effects of the bomb on the people of Hiroshima, see John Hersey, *Hiroshima* (New York: Knopf, 1946); M. Hachiya, *Hiroshima Diary* (Chapel Hill: University of North Carolina Press, 1955); and Masuji Ibuse, *Black Rain* (Tokyo: Kodansha International, 1959). See also the moving descriptions of the bombing by children compiled by Akira Osada as *Children of the A-Bomb* (Tokyo: Uchida, 1959). The fullest report is Committee for the Compilation of Materials on Damage Caused by the Atomic Bombs, *Hiroshima and Nagasaki: The Physical, Medical, and Social Effects of the Atomic Bombings* (New York: Basic Books, 1981).

A good starting point for the debate about the morality of the Hiroshima bombing is the articles in *The Great Decision*, ed. John C. Baker

(New York: Holt, Rinehart, Winston, 1968). Some of the historical data essential to informed judgment are in Herbert Feis, *The Atomic Bomb and the End of World War II* (Princeton, NJ: Princeton University Press, 1966). See also Rufus E. Miles, "The Strange Myth of a Million Lives Saved," *International Security* 10, no.2 (Fall 1985): 121–140.

For Truman's radio announcement of Hiroshima, see *The Truman Administration: A Documentary History*, ed. Barton J. Bernstein (New York: Harper and Row, 1966). The Bernstein text of the quote says "important military base," but on the tape of the broadcast Truman omits "important."

Revolutionary War and Counterinsurgency Tactics

Books on counterinsurgency include John McCuen, *The Art of Counter-Revolutionary War: The Strategy of Counterinsurgency* (Harrisburg, PA: Stackpole, 1966); Carl Leiden and Karl Schmitt, *The Politics of Violence* (Englewood Cliffs, NJ: Prentice Hall, 1968); Julian Paget, *Counterinsurgency Operations* (New York: Walker, 1967); Walter Laqueur, *Guerrilla: A Historical and Critical Study* (Boston: Little, Brown, 1976); Douglas Bluefarb, *The Counterinsurgency Era: U.S. Doctrine and Performance* (New York: Free Press, 1977). Books on specific counterinsurgencies include Frances Lucille Starner, *Magsaysay and the Philippine Peasantry* (Berkeley: University of California Press, 1961); Sir Robert Thompson, *Defeating Communist Insurgency: The Lesson of Malaya and Vietnam* (New York: Praeger, 1966); John Talbott, *The War Without a Name: France in Algeria* (London: Faber and Faber, 1981).

Torture. The most discussed use of torture as a counterinsurgency tactic is the use of torture by the French Army in Algeria. See Talbott, *The War Without a Name*, Ch. 5.

One of the few interesting discussions of this subject by a philosopher is Henry Shue, "Torture," *Philosophy and Public Affairs* 7, no. 2 (Winter 1978): 124–144.

Assassination. A collection of essays on this subject by philosophers is *Assassination*, ed. Harold Zellner (Cambridge, MA: Schenkman, 1974).

War Crimes and Command Responsibility: The Massacre at My Lai

For the experience of American soldiers in Vietnam, see Ron Kovic, *Born on the Fourth of July* (New York: McGraw-Hill, 1977); Philip Caputo, *A Rumor of War* (New York: Holt, Rinehart, and Winston, 1977); Tim O'Brien, *Going After Cacciato* (New York: Delacorte Press, 1978); James Webb, *Fields of Fire* (New York: Bantam Books, 1979); Michael Herr, *Dispatches* (New York: Avon, 1980); Al Santoli, *Everything We Had* (New York: Random House, 1981).

The premier journalistic account of My Lai is Seymour Hersh, *My Lai 4* (New York: Random House, 1970). The Army's official report is summarized in W. R. Peers, *The Mylai Inquiry* (New York: Norton, 1979). Calley's own views are in *Lt. Calley: His Own Story* (as told to John Sack) (New York: Vintage, 1971). See also Richard Hammer, *The Court Martial of Lt. Calley* (New York: Coward McCann, 1971).

For questions of responsibility at My Lai, see Telford Taylor, *Nuremberg and Vietnam: An American Tragedy* (Chicago: Quadrangle, 1970); Alfred Rubin, "Legal Aspects of the My Lai Incident" (1970), Richard Falk, "Son My: War Crimes and Individual Responsibility" (1971), "Legal Aspects of the My Lai Incident: A Response to Professor Rubin" (1971), all reprinted in *The Vietnam War and International Law*, III; (Princeton: Princeton University Press, 1972) William Hays Parks, "Command Responsibility for War Crimes," *Military Law Review* 62 (1973), and *The My Lai Massacre and Its Cover-up*, ed. Joseph Goldstein, Burke Marshall, and Jack Schwartz (New York: Free Press, 1979). See also the essays in *Law and Responsibility in Warfare: The Vietnam Experience*, ed. Peter D. Trooboff, (Chapel Hill: University of North Carolina Press, 1975). For other war crimes in Vietnam, see *Against the Crime of Silence: Proceedings of the Russell International War Crimes Tribunal*, ed. John Duffet, (Flanders, NJ: O'Hare Publications, 1968).

Terrorism and Counterterrorism

For analyses of terrorism, see Walter Laqueur, "Interpretations of Terrorism: Fact, Fiction, and Political Science," *Journal of Contemporary History* 12 (1977): 1–42, and *Terrorism* (Boston: Little, Brown, 1977); H. Edward Price, "The Strategy and Tactics of Revolutionary Terrorism," *Comparative Studies in Society and History* 19 (1977): 52–56; Martha Crenshaw Hutchinson, *Revolutionary Terrorism: The FLN in Algeria* (Stanford, CA: Stanford University Press, 1978); David C. Rapaport and Yonah Alexander, *The Morality of Terrorism: Religious and Secular Justification* (New York: Pergamon Press, 1982); Franklin Ford, *Political Murder: From Tyrannicide to Terrorism* (Cambridge, MA: Harvard University Press 1985). For a quasi-official look at terrorism see the *Report of the Vice-President's Task Force on Combating Terrorism* (Washington, DC: U.S. Government Printing Office, February 1986).

For the comparison of state-sponsored terrorism *versus* substate terrorism, see Edward S. Herman, *The Real Terrorist Network* (Boston: South End Press, 1984). The figure of 3,668 civilians killed by terrorists is the CIA figure for sub-state terrorist groups. See *Patterns of International Terrorism, 1980* (Washington, DC: U.S. Government Printing Office, June 1981), p. ii.

The Raid on Entebbe. This account of the Entebbe raid is drawn principally from the *New York Times* and *Facts on File*. One of several journalistic narratives is William Stevenson, *90 Minutes at Entebbe* (New York: Bantam, 1976). See also Yesh'yahu Ben Porat, *Entebbe Rescue* (New York: Delacorte, 1977); and Michael Goldberg, *Namesake* (New Haven: Yale University Press, 1982).

The Raid on Libya. This account of the raid on Libya is drawn from the *New York Times* and *Facts on File*, supplemented by Seymour Hersh, "Target Qaddafi," *New York Times Magazine* (22 February 1987).

The attack on Libya is defended in Robert Oakley, "International Terrorism," *Foreign Affairs* 65, no.3 (December 1986). Other authors recommending a hard line against terrorism are George Shultz, address at the Park Avenue Synagogue, 25 October 1984, reprinted in *Terrorism*, ed. Bonnie Szumski (St. Paul, MN: Greenhaven, 1986); Robert H. Kupperman, "Terrorism and Public Policy: Domestic Impacts, International Threats," in *American Violence and Public Policy*, ed. Lynn A. Curtis (New Haven: Yale University Press, 1985); and the authors in *Terrorism: How the West Can Win*, ed. Benzion Netanyahu (New York: Farrar, Strauss, Giroux, 1986). A wider-ranging approach is suggested by George Ball in "Shultz Was Wrong on Terrorism," *New York Times* (16 December 1984).

Some of the more interesting post-Libya studies are Christopher H. Pyle, "Defining Terrorism," *Foreign Policy* 64 (Fall 1986): 63–78; Richard L. Rubenstein, *Alchemists of Revolution: Terrorism in the Modern World* (New York: Basic Books, 1987); Walter Reich, "How the President Can Thwart Terror," *New York Times* (19 February 1987); Jeffrey D. Simon, "Misunderstanding Terrorism," *Foreign Policy* 67 (Summer 1987): 104–120.

5
NUCLEAR WAR AND NUCLEAR DETERRENCE

---

1. THE ELEMENTS OF A NUCLEAR WEAPONS POLICY

When the American atomic bomb exploded over Hiroshima, the streets were crowded with adults on their way to work, children on their way to school. Within seconds, tens of thousands of people were incinerated by the fireball or crushed by the atomic blast. Within hours, tens of thousands more died from the firestorm that consumed the city. Within days, thousands more died from the effects of ionizing radiation produced by nuclear fission. Many who survived left Hiroshima in little bands, walking speechlessly away from a city that had ceased to exist.

The bomb that fell on Hiroshima had an explosive force of about 12,000 tons of TNT. The nuclear warhead on the American Minuteman II missile has an explosive force of 1.2 million tons of TNT, 100 times the force of the Hiroshima bomb, and the United States has 450 such missiles. Since Hiroshima in 1945, the Soviet Union (1949), Great Britain (1952), France (1960), China (1964), and India (1974) have developed nuclear weapons, and Israel and South Africa probably have them in storage. In the world's arsenals there are currently more than 60,000 nuclear weapons. To deliver these weapons, the nuclear powers have developed strategic bombers, strategic fighter bombers, land-based intercontinental missiles, submarine-launched intercontinental missiles, air-, land-, and sea-based cruise missiles, shorter-range rockets, nuclear cannon, and even hand-planted nuclear mines. Under current technology, the intercontinental missiles, once launched, cannot be recalled or intercepted. In 30 minutes or less, any city in the world could become another Hiroshima. Indeed, the two superpowers each possess enough nuclear weapons to destroy all the world's cities many times over, and civilization along with them.

It is against this dark background of unprecedented destruction that policies for nuclear weapons must be judged. Citizens in every nation capable of producing or acquiring nuclear weapons must decide: Should we acquire nuclear weapons? If so, what kinds should we develop? What plans should we formulate for using them? In particular, in what circumstances should nuclear weapons be used? against what targets? with what rate of fire? A set of answers to such questions constitutes a *nuclear weapons policy*.

2. THE COUNTERVAILING STRATEGY DEFENDED

The current nuclear weapons policy of the United States, adopted by Gerald Ford in 1974 and revised by Jimmy Carter in 1980, has come to be called "The Countervailing Strategy." The basic goals of the Countervailing Strategy are to deter military aggression by the Soviet Union (a) against the United States, (b) against American allies, (c) in the area around the Persian Gulf. According to the strategy's supporters, the aggressive character of the Soviet regime is manifest in its ideology of revolution; its vast military expenditures; its absorption of reluctant minorities—Ukrainians, Latvians, Estonians, and others—into the Soviet state; its political and military domination of eastern Europe; its invasions of Hungary, Czechoslovakia, and Afghanistan; and its military meddlings in several African states. The technique of the Countervailing Strategy is to demonstrate to the Soviets that whatever gains they might obtain from a military attack on the United States or its allies or in the Persian Gulf will be more than offset by losses they will sustain from American retaliation. In military terms, if there is war between the superpowers, the Countervailing Strategy seeks to guarantee that the United States will win.

To achieve these goals, the United States must have forces that can ride out a Soviet nuclear attack, and still enable the United States to retaliate and inflict unacceptable damage on the Soviet Union. Thus American forces must be hidden and dispersed, and dispersal is achieved by distributing nuclear weapons among bombers, land missiles, and submarines. To prevail in nuclear war, however, requires more than inflicting "unacceptable" retaliatory damage. The United States must plan to retaliate in ways that will impose military defeat on the Soviets, without blowing ourselves up in the process and without encouraging the Soviets to blow us up in return.

Since the Soviets are capable of many different types of aggression, diverse counterattack plans must be developed, each tailored to a specific Soviet act: not so small as to appear weak, not so big as to provoke further conflict. If the Soviets respond to an American response by moving to a higher level of military force, the United States must be prepared to meet and prevail at that higher level, in a measured manner that makes the Soviets regret their escalation, without provoking them to further and more intense attacks. Thus the Countervailing Strategy requires what strategists call escalation dominance, and escalation dominance requires nuclear weapons of all sizes, from the very small to the very big: battlefield nuclear weapons like the Lance missile, "theater" nuclear weapons like the Pershing II, and the big intercontinental missiles like the MX to dominate the highest levels of escalation.

Finally, if the United States is to prevail in a nuclear war with the Soviet Union, the United States needs weapons that can destroy as many Soviet weapons as possible, before they are used against the United States. The United States also needs weapons that can destroy the communications systems that the Soviets need in order to wage war. These "damage limitation" missions require powerful and precise missiles like the MX land missile and the D-5 submarine-based missile, and special space weapons to attack Soviet satellites as well.

The Countervailing Strategy is a grim business. Given Soviet superiority in conventional forces, the Countervailing Strategy calls for the use of American nuclear weapons against the Soviets, *even if the Soviets have not used them first.* By endorsing "first use," it practically guarantees that any war between the two superpowers will be a nuclear war. In many military circumstances, it calls for massive uses of American nuclear weapons, uses that will have widespread destructive side effects. But the main aim of the Countervailing Strategy of "peace through nuclear strength" is not to win a nuclear war but to prevent Soviet aggression, and if Soviet aggression is prevented, there will be no nuclear war.

According to its supporters, history shows that the strategy works. The Soviet Union has not attacked the United States or any ally of the United States, and no nuclear weapon has been used in war since 1945. True, not all the features of the Countervailing Strategy have been part of American planning since 1945. But the basic idea of preventing Soviet expansion through the threat to wage nuclear war has guided American policy at least since Truman broke the Soviet blockade of Berlin in 1948. Given the immense peril of nuclear war, any change in a policy that has produced 40 years of nuclear peace should be viewed with suspicion.

The arguments for the Countervailing Strategy are not all military. Since a nuclear war would be very bad for the human race, whatever prevents a nuclear attack on the United States serves the common interest of mankind, not just American national interests.

Furthermore, nations have a right to defend themselves against aggression. Since nuclear missiles cannot be intercepted once they are launched, this right to self-defense implies a right to threaten counter-attacks, which are the only way to prevent those missiles from being launched in the first place.

The United States concedes the same right of nuclear self-defense to the Soviet Union. The United States made no attempt to stop the development of Soviet nuclear weapons and nuclear bombers, and in 1972 the United States agreed not to construct a national antiballistic missile (ABM) system. In effect the ABM agreement permits the Soviets to destroy the United States, should the Americans attack them first. This is an irrefutable guarantee to the Soviets that the United States will not be the first to attack.

If the Countervailing Strategy looks morally suspicious because of its essential reliance on nuclear threats, its supporters argue that the principal alternatives—Strategic Defense, Finite Deterrence, and Nuclear Disarmament—are morally far worse.

According to supporters of the status quo, while the Countervailing Strategy respects the right of the Soviets to nuclear self-defense, Strategic Defense—the so-called Star Wars system—will prevent the Soviets from exercising that right. It will permit the United States to inflict nuclear risks on others while refusing to accept those risks itself.

In the eyes of the Countervailing Strategy, Finite Deterrence—the retention of just a few American nuclear weapons to be used as a last resort in the face of Soviet nuclear attack—provides no protection against Soviet *non*nuclear aggression. In the face of nuclear aggression, its only recourse (assuming a small American nuclear stockpile) is an attack on Soviet cities. Unlike the Countervailing Strategy, Finite Deterrence makes Soviet citizens hostages to American nuclear weapons: in effect, it commits kidnapping before the war starts and follows with murder after war breaks out.

Unilateral Nuclear Disarmament—giving up nuclear weapons while the Soviets retain theirs—is not only unfair to the United States, but it would permit the Soviet aggressors to blackmail the United States into submission on any point in dispute—so the argument goes. If the United States threatened to use nonnuclear weapons, the Soviets could always respond with nuclear threats and, given the power of nuclear weapons, these threats would always succeed. Instead of collapsing before threats, the Countervailing Strategy responds with measured, believable counterthreats.

The Countervailing Strategy is a tough strategy, but nuclear weapons have created a tough world, and they cannot be disinvented. The result of 40 years of adjustments, the Countervailing Strategy is, according to its defenders, the only morally appropriate response to the post-Hiroshima world.

Criticisms have been launched at the Countervailing Strategy from the political right and left. Critics on the left worry principally about the risks the strategy inflicts on innocent parties around the world. Critics on the right worry mainly about the risks it inflicts on Americans.

3. CRITICISMS OF THE COUNTERVAILING STRATEGY FROM THE RIGHT

(a)   Critics on the right focus on the disturbing fact that the Countervailing Strategy leaves the United States defenseless against Soviet attack. Should the Soviets choose to launch a nuclear strike against the United States, under the Countervailing Strategy the United States would be destroyed. The Countervailing Strategy operates via threats of counterattack—in other words, through nuclear deterrence. But deterrence is not the same thing as a physical defense that the enemy cannot penetrate no matter what he thinks or does. Deterrence depends for its success on the psychological intimidation of Soviet leaders, and these leaders might choose not to be intimidated. Deterrence, even nuclear deterrence, places the safety of the American people in the hands of the Soviets. If there is a right to self-defense, deterrence does not satisfy that right.

(b)   The current vulnerability of the United States to nuclear attack implies that the Countervailing Strategy does not provide escalation dominance against an opponent that wants to destroy the United States even at the cost of its own destruction. Lack of escalation dominance makes it impossible for the United States to make credible nuclear threats, and lack of credible nuclear threats allows the Soviets to use their superior conventional military strength to defend their interests and spread their influence around the world. Lack of ability to dominate in nuclear war may cause the United States to lose the cold war without a shot being fired. This is not only bad for the United States; it is bad for nations falling under Soviet influence. American influence in the world is not invariably benign. But when measured by moral values, it is morally superior to Soviet influence.

(c)   Military leaders note that the Countervailing Strategy is essentially a strategy of retaliation, and a strict strategy of retaliation leaves the military initiative in the hands of the enemy. From the military point of view, if there is going to be war, it is far better to seize the initiative and strike first, especially in a nuclear age, when striking first may be the only way to save the United States from annihilation. Given the aggressive tendencies of the Soviet Union and the deep ideological differences between the Soviets and the Americans, deterrence will not last forever. When deterrence breaks down, all Americans, even those who are presently doves, will grasp the logic of striking first.

(d)   The Countervailing Strategy attempts to provide deterrence, not defense, but there is some reason to think that it cannot even provide deterrence. Through the 1970s, the Soviets developed powerful and accurate missiles with multiple warheads. These weapons put American land-based missiles and other locatable assets at increased risk from Soviet attack. With advances in air defense, antisubmarine warfare, and ballistic missile defense, the Soviets have put all American strategic weapons at risk, and may have deprived the United States of the ability to retaliate against nuclear attack.

(e)   The Countervailing Strategy commits the United States to the use of tactical and theater nuclear weapons in the event of a Soviet attack against western Europe. The use—or anticipated use—of American theater nuclear weapons, presumably against the Soviet homeland, would substantially increase the chances of a Soviet strike against the United States. But it is irresponsible of Western leaders to risk the survival of the United States on behalf of nations that are capable of conducting their own defense. It is unfair to the American people to put them at risk to assist Germany and Japan, which have—to say the least—no history of service that puts the United States in their debt.

4.   THE CASE FOR STRATEGIC DEFENSE

The criticisms from the right against the Countervailing Strategy lead naturally to proposals for replacing deterrence with Strategic Defense. Strategic defenses are systems for intercepting and destroying Soviet nuclear weapons before they land on the United States. Proposals for strategic defense date back to the 1950s, when antibomber surface-to-air missiles were deployed around the United States and when work on anti-ballistic missile (ABM) systems was begun. By the late 1960s, both the Soviet Union and the United States had developed partially effective antimissile systems, designed to shoot down missiles as they approached the ground. But a "partially effective" strategic defense provides little safety in an age when a single bomb can kill 20 million people, and both sides agreed by treaty to stop the race in ABM systems in 1972.

In the late 1970s, the increasing vulnerability of land ICBMs, combined with technological innovations in computers, new remote sensing and tracking devices, and new ways of attacking missiles, revived interest in strategic defense. In 1983, a major research effort in this direction was inaugurated by President Reagan. The system of strategic defense projected by the Reagan administration for the late 1990s involves laser attacks on Soviet missiles in the boost phase as they come up, various types of attacks in the midcourse phase, and further attacks in the terminal (descent) phase, perhaps with solid projectiles that crash into enemy missiles.

The difficulties of knocking down 1,000 or 2,000 missiles and perhaps 10,000 separable warheads, mixed in among thousands of decoys, in less than 30 minutes, are formidable. Since the system could never be tested under wartime conditions, one could never be confident that it would knock down all or nearly all incoming enemy missiles. But supporters of strategic defenses argue that we could be reasonably confident that the system would work, and certainly the Soviets could never be confident that it wouldn't.

Furthermore, suppose that the system "failed," and shot down only 50 percent of incoming enemy missiles in a large attack. With half the enemy missiles gone, the United States would surely retain enough of its strategic forces and communications systems to launch a devastating counterstrike: strategic defenses, in short, would deny to any adversary the chance to launch a "decapitating" nuclear first strike against the United States. If 50 percent of enemy missiles were shot down before they reached the United States, 50 million rather than 100 million Americans might die from the attack. Any ABM system that lets 50 million Americans die has failed. But even in failure the system will have saved 50 million lives.

This argument assumes a large attack on the United States. But suppose that only a small attack is launched, or a single missile heads toward the United States by accident, or a single missile is launched at us by terrorists. Currently, such events might kill millions of Americans. But even a small system of strategic defense could shoot down one or two missiles, and everyone would be saved.

Strategic defenses do not threaten people; they threaten only nuclear weapons. They constitute a system of true defense, not a system of deterrence, and are justified by the right of self-defense. People of all political persuasions must agree that anything which destroys nuclear weapons on their way to targets cannot be morally bad.

5. THE CASE AGAINST STRATEGIC DEFENSE

(a) The argument that strategic defenses might save 50 million American lives starts by positing a Soviet attack and then imagines that 50 percent of the attack will be wiped out by defenses that are 50 percent effective. But it is a mistake to assume that the presence of American strategic defenses will not affect the size of the incoming Soviet attack. If the Americans construct defenses that are 50 percent effective, then the Soviets can achieve the same level of destruction as before by shooting off twice as many missiles. No strategic defense can prevent them from doing this. True, it will cost the Soviets money to fire twice as many missiles, but it will cost us even more to try and stop them. Unless a shield is 100 percent effective, it cannot protect the United States from total destruction by ballistic missiles.

No one believes that a 100 percent effective defense against ballistic missiles can be constructed. But suppose that one could be. Would the United States cease to be vulnerable to nuclear attack? Not at all, since nuclear weapons can be delivered not just on missiles but also on bombers or cruise missiles or small boats. They can be put on mines in harbors, or even delivered in luggage. Of all nuclear weapons policies, admittedly only Strategic Defense attempts to rescue the United States from the condition of nuclear vulnerability. But there is little point in making an attempt that is bound to fail on its own terms.

(b)   The publicized purpose of Strategic Defense is to blunt a nuclear sneak attack—or "first strike"—by the Soviet Union. But any system that can stop a Soviet first strike will be even more effective in stopping a Soviet *second* strike—the missiles that the Soviets would direct back against the United States should they suffer an American first strike.

Consider the military position of the Soviet Union should American defenses be constructed and should the United States choose to attack. The war begins as American anti-satellite weapons, launched from F-15 fighters, destroy Soviet warning systems and communications satellites. With Soviet satellites blinded, the United States launches its fleet of highly accurate MX and Trident D-5 missiles, pulverizing Soviet ICBM fields, while superaccurate cruise missiles seek out and destroy Soviet command and control centers. Meanwhile, American ships, subs, helicopters, and planes hunt down Soviet strategic submarines, tracked continuously from their "choke points" as they exit the Baltic Sea, the Black Sea, and the Sea of Japan, and destroy them with nuclear depth charges. The few surviving Soviet missiles remain unfired or are picked off by the American Star Wars defenses.

All the weaponry in this American first strike plan currently exists—except the strategic defenses. Thus, effective strategic defenses would deprive the Soviets of their ability to deter American attacks with threats of retaliation. This loss of deterrent capability will increase Russian insecurity, a sense of insecurity well buttressed by recollections of previous "first strikes" by the Mongols (1238), the French (1812), the British and Americans (1918), the Poles (1920), and the Germans (1941). Deprived of their ability to launch an effective second strike, the Soviets in a crisis might feel that they must use their nuclear weapons in the only effective way left open to them—a first strike against the United States. Instead of decreasing the Soviet threat, a Star Wars system actually increases it.

(c)   If the United States succeeds in constructing partially effective strategic defenses, the Soviet Union will follow suit. Then each side will have deprived the other of the capacity to retaliate in a second strike. Each side will know that if it strikes first, it can will a nuclear war; if it waits, it will surely lose. Each side will suspect the other of trying to strike first, and each side will feel forced to strike as quickly as possible. Strategic defenses on both sides virtually guarantee that every crisis between the superpowers will develop into nuclear war.

(d)   Since 1945, the main function of nuclear weapons has not been to fight wars but to make threats. The United States directed nuclear threats at the Soviet Union during the Iran crisis in 1946, the Berlin block-ade in 1948, the Cuban missile crisis in 1962, the Vietnam War in 1969, and the Yom Kippur War in 1973. In general these threats have been less efficacious than one might expect, mainly because the opposing side did not believe that they would be carried out. Confronted, for example, with Nixon's threat (conveyed through Kissinger) to use nuclear weapons against North Vietnam and perhaps against Russia in 1969, the Soviets correctly surmised that the Americans would not attack North Vietnam with nuclear weapons for fear of suffering nuclear retaliation. The Amer-ican bluff was called.

Since the Soviets achieved nuclear parity with the United States in the early 1970s, the frequency of American nuclear threats has diminished. The construction of strategic defenses, which might give the United States the ability to win a nuclear war, would restore credibility to American nuclear threats, and the practice of nuclear threats might revive. This would give the United States some ability to control Soviet behavior. But it would also increase the probability of nuclear war, a risk not worth taking for small gains obtainable in safer ways.

(e) The supporters of strategic defense argue that strategic defenses—true defenses—are grounded in the right to self-defense in a way that the Countervailing Strategy is not. If they are justified by self-defense, it follows, on this view, that we are obliged to build them. But suppose it is true that the United States has the *right* to build strategic defenses. It does not follow from this that the United States is obliged to build them, since no one is obliged to do everything that he has a right to do. We have at all times a right to express our ideas. It does not follow that we are obliged to express them, and that we would be wicked if we kept silent. Likewise, no right to self-defense can make strategic defense morally obligatory. It is part of the logic of rights that we always have a right not to do what we have a right to do.

6. CRITICISMS OF THE COUNTERVAILING STRATEGY FROM THE LEFT

(a) The Countervailing Strategy makes assumptions about history, especially recent history, for which there is less evidence than most Amer-icans think.

The Countervailing Strategy assumes that American readiness to use nuclear weapons has produced 40 years of peace in Europe. This presumes there would have been war in Europe if the United States had not had nuclear weapons. But it is impossible to guess what might have happened in Europe if the United States had deployed only conventional weapons, and impossible to show that fear of nuclear war has produced 40 years of

European peace. Europe had 40 years of peace after the Franco-Prussian War of 1871, in days when there were no nuclear weapons and when governments in general were more militaristic than they are now. Both world wars were disasters in Europe, and those terrible lessons help to prevent war, nuclear weapons or no nuclear weapons. Beside, since 1945 the industrialized nations have realized that, given technological innovation, internal development does not require external conquest. Fear of conventional war, the division of Germany, the decline in militaristic political movements, and general prosperity have all contributed as much to peace in Europe as has fear of nuclear war.

The Countervailing Strategy appropriates the popular view of the Soviets as aggressors. But though Soviet propaganda is revolutionary, the Soviet leaders are old and conservative, especially in military matters. In the historical record, the Russians are rarely aggressors, and when they are, as in the Crimean War, they invariably lose. Since 1945, the main thrust of Soviet military action has been not to support aggressive change but to restore and preserve the status quo. The incorporation of the Baltic states, for example, restores those countries to the condition they were in 1917. The Warsaw Pact (i.e. Soviet) invasions of Hungary, Czechoslovakia, and Afghanistan were in each case undertaken to restore a pro-Soviet regime to power. Soviet domination in eastern Europe, which includes domination of former allies of Nazi Germany, is a result of the unique circumstances that ended World War II, and provides no proof of plans for further conquest. There is little indication that the Soviets, at present or at any time since 1945, planned the military invasion of any western European nation. It is absurd to suggest that the Soviets, who spent millions constructing a pipeline to sell natural gas in West Germany, would set about blowing up their customers the minute the United States stopped issuing nuclear threats.

(b)   The Countervailing Strategy calls for the use of tactical and theater nuclear weapons in the face of Soviet conventional attack. The Soviets would probably respond in kind, and even if they did not, the use of these weapons on the crowded plains of Europe would kill millions of citizens in nations the tactical nuclear weapons are supposed to protect. Indeed, the destruction caused by nuclear weapons on the battlefield is so great that it is problematic whether permission for their use would ever be granted. The threat to use these weapons is incredible, and their actual use is suicidal.

The standard argument for deploying tactical nuclear weapons is "superior Soviet conventional strength." But the nonnuclear military resources of the NATO states outclass the Soviet Union, and the Soviets cannot muster anything like the 3:1 ratio of forces military experts claim is needed for successful invasion. The Soviets cannot depend on the loyalty of eastern European troops and must maintain a military presence along the long Chinese border as well. Furthermore, current military trends—

precision antitank weapons, for example—generally favor defense over offense. All these factors show that the Countervailing Strategy's reliance on tactical and theater nuclear weapons is outdated and dangerous.

(c)   If there is any consolation the student can draw from military history since 1945, it is that the political leaders of nuclear nations have been exceedingly reluctant to use nuclear weapons. The French refused an American offer of nuclear weapons during the Indochina war in 1954, the same year in which Eisenhower tabled a recommendation from a subcommittee of the Joint Chiefs of Staff calling for a nuclear attack on Russia before the Soviets could develop intercontinental strategic bombers. The Soviets considered and backed off from a preemptive, presumably nuclear, strike against China in 1969. The nonuse of nuclear weapons for over 40 years has generated a nuclear taboo that is one of the world's best safeguards against nuclear holocaust. In military planning, safety demands that the nuclear threshold—the point at which a military conflict moves from the conventional stage to the nuclear stage—be set as high as possible. By calling for a first use of nuclear weapons in the early stages of superpower conflict, the Countervailing Strategy ignores the nuclear taboo and lowers the nuclear threshold.

(d)   The key idea of the Countervailing Strategy is to issue a measured "countervailing" response to every Soviet initiative. The execution of these measured responses assumes that the president and his generals will be able to control the course of an ongoing nuclear war, using strategic weapons with restraint and precision. Many experts doubt that this can be done. It is not merely that Soviet submarine-based missiles can destroy Washington seven minutes after launch, probably killing the president and all his potential successors. The problem is that each large nuclear explosion produces an electromagnetic pulse that will destroy computers and communications systems for hundreds—perhaps thousands—of miles around.

The Countervailing Strategy also assumes that strategic weapons, once launched, will strike their targets precisely, and that the Soviets, suffering these strikes, will be forced to realize that further responses are futile. But it is dubious that in such circumstances rational Soviet heads will prevail. Suppose the Soviets launched a measured and precise attack against American strategic installations, wiping out most American strategic weapons, but incidentally killing several million American citizens. Could the Soviets expect that American leaders would decide that response is futile and that no counterattack should be launched to avenge these deaths? Would they not be fools to expect American surrender? Isn't the Countervailing Strategy equally foolish in expecting surrender from Soviet leaders in similar circumstances?

Many liberal critics of the Countervailing Strategy believe that the most likely result of any use of strategic weapons by either superpower is escalation to a massive nuclear exchange that would destroy both countries.

(e)   One crucial element in the Countervailing Strategy is "damage limitation," designed, as Caspar Weinberger put it, "to end the war on favorable terms." "Damage limitation" in nuclear war consists mainly in preemptive strikes against the nuclear weapons of the opponent. Such strikes against the hardest of targets require nuclear missiles of great accuracy and great explosive force, firing multiple warheads to assure that if one warhead misses, the others will destroy the target. Such highly accurate multiple-warhead missiles, like the land-based MX and the sea-based D-5, introduce an element of instability in relations between the superpowers. The Soviets, worrying about the MX and its 10 warheads, might think that their missiles are in peril, and might be prompted to fire their weapons for fear of losing them in an American attack. Firing their missiles, they will necessarily consider American MXs choice targets, since a Soviet warhead striking an MX will destroy 10 American warheads: a 10 to 1 exchange. The Americans, thinking that the Soviets are thinking this, will feel pressured to use the MX before losing it to Soviet attack. In general, precise "counterforce" weapons like the MX connote "damage limitation" to those who possess them but "preemptive strike" to those at whom they are aimed.

(f)   The Countervailing Strategy requires that American weapons be better than Soviet weapons, not merely equal to them. The Soviets, for their part, want American weapons to be no better than their own. Thus the Countervailing Strategy provokes a strategic arms race, in which the Americans innovate and the Soviets respond, or the Soviets innovate and the Americans respond. For example, the Soviet ABM of 1967 provoked the American MIRV of 1969, which provoked the Soviet MIRV of 1974, which provoked new interest in an American ABM and the Star Wars proposal of 1983.

Though it consumes only a fraction of the overall defense budget, American spending on strategic arms under the Countervailing Strategy is exceedingly expensive compared with discretionary spending on social welfare and education. Furthermore, spending on complex strategic weapons diverts scientific talent from basic research and from the development of consumer products and services. But the most negative feature of the strategic arms race is that the development of ever more complex strategic systems raises the risk of accidental nuclear war.

The *Challenger* and Chernobyl disasters of 1986 show that the most carefully supervised technology of both superpowers is subject to catastrophic failure. Most specialists agree that the chance of accidental nuclear war resulting from either a mechanical or a human failure is quite small, and that the chance of a deliberate or accidental launch of nuclear weapons is also quite small—in normal circumstances. But the chance of accidental nuclear war will increase substantially in the case of a crisis between the superpowers, and the chances of accident are proportionately greater when the technology is new than when it is tried and true.

Some experts doubt that the strategic systems of the superpowers could maintain a state of peace during an extended, full-fledged nuclear alert. The systems might go off by accident, or commanders in the field or at central posts might be prompted to fire off weapons before the system breaks down. At least in times of international crisis, the two strategic systems of the superpowers, summed together, might become a single self-detonating doomsday machine.

(g)   The main moral argument for the Countervailing Strategy is that it is sustained by the right to self-defense. Most people subscribe to the right to self-defense, and when they do so, they have a clear idea in mind of the sort of situation in which this right applies. The paradigm case, perhaps, is the person threatened by a mugger with a gun who shoots the mugger with a gun of his own. To the degree that a situation differs from this paradigm case, the applicability of the "right to self-defense" becomes more and more questionable.

Obviously there are many differences between a street mugging and the present confrontation between the superpowers.

(i)   The paradigm case assigns the right to self-defense to an individual person; defenders of the Countervailing Strategy assign it to a nation-state. But to speak of the rights of nonindividuals leads into muddy waters: do business corporations, for example, have a right to life and a right to self-defense?

(ii)   In the paradigm case, force is used to stop the mugging in progress; in the nuclear case, force is to be used not to stop a nuclear attack but to make the Soviets regret what they have already done. This is more like punishment than self-defense.

(iii)   In the paradigm case, force is directed at the attacker and injures only the attacker. In the Countervailing Strategy, force is directed at the attacker but injures many innocent bystanders. Moral philosophers disagree on the extent to which it is permissible to injure bystanders in the course of self-defense. Suppose that one could shoot back at the mugger, but only by shooting through the body of a bystander the mugger has seized as a shield. Would it be permissible to shoot? Would it be morally permissible to shoot through *ten* bystanders? Studies show that many limited nuclear attack patterns under the Countervailing Strategy, though directed at military targets, will kill millions of noncombatant bystanders, both in the Soviet Union and in countries not allied with either super-power.

Though nuclear attacks under the Countervailing Strategy are not, to use Elliot Richardson's phrase, aimed at "cities as such," the side effects of American nuclear attacks will probably destroy cities and will certainly kill many civilians. The threat of such collateral destruction, according to the strategy, is one of the things that deters the Soviets from attacking us. Thus the collateral damage serves our purposes; it is one of the means by which we achieve the ends of deterrence. But actions that are means to an end are always intended actions. Thus, although American missiles are not aimed at cities, the mass killing of civilians and the destruction of cities is an intended part of the Countervailing Strategy.

Thus, the Countervailing Strategy is like telling a mugger that if he does not break off his attack, you will surely kill not only him but his daughter as well. Such a threat, if executed, is hardly justifiable on grounds of self-defense, and if the daughter dies, most juries would call it murder.

In sum, then, the critics of the left view the Countervailing Strategy as unnecessary, dangerous, technically unimplementable, expensive, risky, unstable, and immoral. It lowers the nuclear threshold and provokes an arms race. Critics who take this line against the Countervailing Strategy propose two alternatives: Finite Deterrence and Unilateral Nuclear Disarmament. Both of these policies take issue with the Countervailing Strategy about the very nature of nuclear bombs.

7. TWO VIEWS ABOUT ATOMIC BOMBS

The Countervailing Strategy integrates nuclear weapons into the American fighting plans. It treats nuclear weapons as genuine weapons that can, and should, be used in time of war. On this theory, nuclear weapons are an important source of military strength, and in any serious conflict between nuclear superpowers, it is inevitable that nuclear weapons will be used. Viewed as trump cards in battle, nuclear weapons have been dispersed worldwide, and they are ready for use by all the services—even the Marines It follows from this attitude that the military services must plan for the use of nuclear weapons in battle *even if the other side has not used them first.* The armed services were secretly instructed by Dwight Eisenhower in 1953: "In the event of hostilities, the United States will consider nuclear weapons to be as available for use as other munitions."

Supporters of the view that nuclear weapons are simply bombs argue that the main effects of nuclear bombs are terrible but not unique. More people died in the bombing of Dresden in February 1945 and in the bombing of Tokyo in March 1945 than died at Hiroshima or Nagasaki. The main effect of a nuclear weapon is an explosion, and explosions have been a central feature of warfare since the introduction of gunpowder in the late Middle Ages. Of course, it is terrible to use atomic bombs against cities, but they need not be so used. Dwight Eisenhower said at a press conference in 1955, "In any combat where these things can be used on strictly military targets I see no reason why they shouldn't be used exactly as you would use a bullet or anything else." Indeed, the explosive charges on the smallest nuclear weapons are smaller than the explosive charges on the conventional "blockbuster" bombs of World War II.

But the majority of people since Hiroshima have sensed that there is something special and terrible about nuclear weapons. The blinding flash, the great heat, the tremendous mushroom cloud, the enveloping firestorm create destruction on such a scale that nuclear destruction seems different from "ordinary" mass destruction. The first news reporter to fly over Nagasaki wrote:

> Burned, blasted, and scarred, Nagasaki looked like a city of death. . . . This is destruction of a sort never before imagined by man and therefore is almost indescribable. The area where the bomb hit is absolutely flat and only the markings of the building foundations provide a clue as to what may have been in the area before the energy of the universe was turned loose. (W. H. Lawrence, "Dead Nagasaki Seen from a B-17")

The special character of nuclear weapons in the foundation and focus of the policies of Finite Deterrence and Nuclear Disarmament. According to these policies, nuclear weapons are not really weapons at all, but instruments of mass destruction that have no rational military use. In addition to the vast quantitative destruction promised by nuclear war, Finite Deterrence theorists and unilateral nuclear disarmers propose six additional arguments for the special character of nuclear weapons.

First, nuclear weapons used in a war might have unique effects on civilization as a whole. A concerted use of these weapons can destroy a whole society; a large-scale nuclear war could destroy civilization itself. Civilization can survive vast destruction; World War II showed that. But there is a level of destruction beyond which civilization cannot survive. Many believe that nuclear war will go beyond this level. True, war with conventional weapons might produce these results. But the destruction of civilization is a likely consequence of a large-scale nuclear war. It is only an unlikely consequence of a conventional war.

Second, nuclear weapons, unlike conventional weapons, produce radiation and radioactive fallout (dust contaminated with radioactive particles, drifting through the stratosphere). Fallout poisons the earth, injures people in nations that have no stake in the quarrel, and affects human genes for generations to come.

Third, a number of scientific experts believe that smoke and dust generated by nuclear explosions will blot out the sun and lower surface temperatures, altering the earth's climate in the short and long run. If this "nuclear winter" hypothesis is correct, a nuclear war of sufficient size might kill several billion people from exposure and starvation. No other weapons have such effects on climate.

Fourth, if a sufficient quantity of radiation is released in a nuclear war, the human species will become extinct. Fortunately, the world's nuclear arsenals are currently too small to achieve this result, and the total explosive force of nuclear arsenals has been diminishing since the 1960s. But it would not be difficult for the superpowers to build up their arsenals to species-threatening levels. Among weapons systems, only biological weapons—special in their own way—have a greater potential to destroy the human race.

Fifth, nuclear weapons are unique in military history in that, when delivered by large missiles, they provide an immense increase in offensive potential with no corresponding increase in defensive capability. When guns and bullets were introduced, an invading army improved its offensive potential. But at the same time, people in the invaded country could use guns and bullets to kill the invaders. With current technology, however, no nation can save itself from mass destruction by an enemy armed with nuclear missiles and determined to use them. A single thermonuclear weapon exploded over New York City will kill 20 million people or more, and even with a Star Wars defense it is impossible to intercept every last warhead in a fleet of enemy missiles. We are all vulnerable before nuclear opponents; every reader of this book might die—in the next minute—from a nuclear attack.

From this fifth fact about nuclear war a sixth fact emerges. In a war between two nuclear powers the likely result is that each will devastate the other. It matters little if one nation is bigger or stronger. The end result is the same for both. A war between nuclear powers must be a war without winners.

Many specialists in nuclear warfare accept these six claims only with reservations. They note that these results follow for large-scale nuclear war, but they may not follow for small-scale nuclear wars. Nuclear weapons can be made small, and there is nothing to prevent a nation from using only a few nuclear weapons in war, not its whole arsenal. But it seems clear that once one nation uses a few small nuclear weapons, the nuclear taboo will be broken and the probability will increase greatly that many large ones will be used. If the effects of a large nuclear war are unique, then even a small nuclear war is a uniquely risky idea.

8. FINITE DETERRENCE

According to Finite Deterrence, nuclear devices are not genuine weapons and they have no military function. They do, however, have one and only one legitimate use, which is to prevent the use of nuclear weapons by the other side. Thus the United States should keep a small stock of nuclear weapons for use as a last resort, after the other side has used them first.

From the principles of Finite Deterrence, it follows—contrary to Eisenhower's directive—that nuclear devices should *not* be "available for use" by the armed services. The battlefield nuclear weapons now in possession of the Army should be decommissioned, as should the Army's short- and medium-range nuclear missiles: the Lance, the Nike-Hercules, the Pershing I, and the Pershing II. (This process is already underway as a result of the Reagan-Gorbachev summit in 1987.) The Navy should remove nuclear weapons from its attack submarines, aircraft carriers, cruisers, destroyers, and frigates, and should not release nuclear weapons to the Marines—as current arrangements provide. The Air Force should remove nuclear weapons from all nuclear equipped tactical aircraft, such as the Phantom, the Eagle, and the Falcon. Any systems that the Army or Navy or Air Force deploys that are "dual capable" (capable of using either conventional or nuclear weapons) such as ground- and sea-launched cruise missiles—should be decommissioned or redesigned so they cannot carry nuclear weapons. Officers and staff involved in strategy and tactics should be instructed by the president not to expect to use nuclear weapons in military encounters, no matter how hard pressed. Finite Deterrence strategists make parallel recommendations for NATO forces in Europe not already covered by these suggestions.

Would the defense of the United States and Europe be jeopardized by such sweeping denuclearization of fighting forces? Consider the *current* military situation. American and NATO forces are instructed to stock all kinds of nuclear weapons and to plan on using them. Yet the authorization for the use of these weapons can come only from the president or his specific delegates. The president may be reluctant to issue the authorization—for fear of nuclear reprisals, for psychological or moral reasons, or because use of the weapons would injure allies more than the enemy. Since 1945 the presidents have made occasional nuclear threats, but no president has come near to authorizing the use of nuclear weapons. So the military services are required to plan on using weapons they may never be allowed to use.

One does not have to be a military expert to see that current arrangements are a battlefield disaster waiting to happen. The addiction of American military forces to nuclear weapons planning may be part of the reason for the services' current ineffectiveness in conventional military operations, as the botched Son Tay, *Mayagüez*, and Tehran rescue attempts, the Beirut barracks catastrophe, the Grenada invasion mix-ups, and the U.S.S. *Stark* debacle all testify. All Finite Deterrence asks is that the military plan on using weapons they actually will use. Once the break from nuclear dependency is accomplished, all the time spent on training personnel to protect and use nuclear weapons could be spent on improving the skills of conventional fighting forces. This will make the armed services more, rather than less, effective.

Could denuclearized NATO forces withstand a Warsaw Pact invasion of the West? The Soviets are alleged to have superior conventional forces, but they cannot rely fully on the troops of their allies, the opposing forces present formidable military problems, and the invasion of the West might provoke revolts in Soviet satellite states. At any rate, there is no reason for NATO forces to tolerate continuing military conditions that increase the chances of Soviet success. Nonnuclear defensive measures may be more expensive then piling up nuclear weapons, but they are a better investment than the purchase of weapons the use of which is a form of suicide.

This leaves the large-scale strategic nuclear weapons. For Finite Deterrence, the guiding principle for strategic weapons is "No first use—no early second use." The United States must never be the first to use nuclear weapons, and should nuclear weapons be used against the United States, the president or his successor must not feel that a second strike need be launched immediately if it is going to be launched at all. The nuclear weapons systems of the United States must be able to ride out a nuclear first strike and be ready for use days and perhaps even weeks after war has commenced.

This should be American policy, and what is more, the United States should demonstrate the existence of the policy with actions and not just with words. It must design strategic systems that cannot rationally be used for a first strike but that can survive to launch a delayed second strike.

It follows that the United States must abandon its antisatellite weapons program, since shooting down satellites is a first step toward a first strike. To assure opponents that their strategic weapons are not targets of an American first strike, American missiles should lack "hard target kill capacity," that is, the ability to strike enemy missile silos and command bunkers accurately enough to destroy them. The United States should abandon all attempts at constructing strategic defenses, since the only feasible use of strategic defenses is to pick off enemy missiles retaliating against an American first strike.

Most important of all, the United States should replace all multiple-warhead missiles with single-warhead missiles, scrapping or retooling the Minuteman III, Poseidon 3-A, MX, and D-5 missiles. The reason for this is evident with a little mathematics. Suppose that two nations have 100 missiles apiece and that each warhead on each missile has a 90 percent chance of destroying an enemy missile if it catches it on the ground. If each nation places one warhead on top of each missile, then if nation A launches all of its missiles at B in a first strike, there is a 99 percent chance that at least one missile from B will survive with the capacity to kill millions of citizens of A in a second strike. On the other hand, suppose that each nation puts ten independently targeted missiles on top of each missile. Then if A attacks B, it is 99 percent probable that A will wipe out *all* of B's missiles, and B will have no power to retaliate. Without multiple warheads, each nation is deterred by the thought of sure retaliation. With multiple warheads, each nation is strongly tempted to destroy all the missiles of the other, before the other destroys its missiles first. This is what Finite Deterrence theorists have in mind when they say that MIRVs (multiple independently targeted reentry vehicles) are "destabilizing" and must be eliminated.

Would all these reductions weaken American defense? If "American defense" means "attacking and destroying the Soviet Union," then these reductions will weaken defense. But for Finite Deterrence, plans to destroy the Soviet Union are immoral and dangerous, and have nothing to do with genuine national defense. If national defense means "increasing the chances of American survival," then these reductions will enhance defense. Large multiple-warhead missiles facilitate American first strikes, and this makes them so threatening that, in a crisis, they might provoke an opponent into a "damage limiting" first strike on the United States. Giving them up will decrease the chance of such Soviet attack, so sacrificing MIRVs actually increases national security.

Once the first-strike-facilitating nuclear devices are removed from the strategic arsenal, Finite Deterrence demands that all the rest should be as invulnerable as possible. Strategic submarines at sea are hidden and dispersed, and the fleet as a whole is invulnerable for the foreseeable future. Thus, the core of the nuclear deterrent should be submarine-based. Two features of current submarine basing, however, need to be changed. The current trend toward fewer and larger submarines should be reversed, as a larger fleet of smaller subs would be more secure. And the current "fail deadly" arrangement, which permits submarine commanders to launch missiles in the absence of certain countervailing commands, should be abandoned and replaced by locked weapons and secure communications, whatever the cost.

Strategic bombers are vulnerable on the ground but less vulnerable in the air. When armed with cruise missiles, they have a better chance of delivering nuclear devices on target, but they also become MIRVed missiles with wings, usable for first strike options if a crisis has brought them close to the enemy border. If strategic bombers are to be retained at all, they should combine advanced penetration technology with a return to shorter-range attack missiles. One argument in favor of retaining at least some strategic bombers is that strategic bombers can be recalled but missiles cannot. (Recallability is consistent with the Finite Deterrence principle of "no early second use.")

Fixed land-based ICBMs are the most vulnerable strategic weapons, and Finite Deterrence theorists generally feel that invulnerability requires that all fixed ICBMs be replaced by smaller, more dispersed, mobile ICBMs, if the United States is to retain ICBMs at all. To guard against accidental, unauthorized, or otherwise regrettable launches, a radio-controlled self-destruct device should be placed on each missile.

It is clear from this outline that Finite Deterrence increases the role of the Navy in nuclear deterrence, while decreasing the roles of the Air Force and the Army. Traditionally such changes arouse fierce resistance, and an uncomfortably large fraction of American strategic planning has been more the result of interservice rivalries than of strict calculation of national needs. To put an end to this irrational competition, Finite Deterrence recommends that all delivery systems for nuclear weapons should be concentrated in a separate military service, under the direct control of the president and the secretary of defense, and disconnected from the Joint Chiefs of Staff. Such an administrative system for nuclear devices is a necessary expression of the concept that nuclear devices are not weapons and should not be available for military use. Only such a system will convince the military that they must learn to rely on conventional weapons, and that nuclear devices are not weapons at all but harbingers of Armageddon.

In sum, Finite Deterrence proposes that the entire stock of deployed nuclear weapons be placed on a fleet of small strategic submarines, mobile ICBMs, and strategic bombers. All missiles will have single warheads, and will remain at all times under the positive control of the president and secretary of defense or their designated successors. These weapons are to be used only in the event of a nuclear attack on the United States, but not necessarily even then.

Should the president choose to launch a second strike, he must choose appropriate responses to nuclear attacks of various kinds. It is sometimes alleged that under Finite Deterrence the president will have so few weapons available that they must be targeted on cities to maximize the destructive efficiency of the reduced nuclear arsenal. But with all nuclear weapons concealed and dispersed, it is highly probable that the president would have several hundred warheads available for a second strike. Directed at enemy military forces, isolated industrial establishments, power stations, dams, and so forth, these warheads could cause enough damage to offset by a large margin anything a potential enemy might hope to gain from an attack on the United States. Furthermore, these forces *could* be directed against enemy cities, and no enemy could be sure that its cities would not be destroyed if it attacked the United States. This capacity, by itself, provides a strong deterrent against nuclear attacks on American cities. Though Finite Deterrence permits the possibility of future Hiroshimas, it does not commit the president in advance to city-destroying second strikes.

9. CRITICISMS OF FINITE DETERRENCE FROM THE RIGHT

(a) Deterrence is an attempt to influence the mind of an opponent, so what is crucial to deterrence is not what you intend but how what you intend to do appears to your opponent. Nuclear weapons are greatly feared, and the removal of nuclear weapons makes military forces less intimidating, regardless of how effective they actually are. Removal of nuclear weapons from NATO and American military forces will increase the chances that those forces will be challenged. If the Soviet challenge begins with conventional weapons, and the Soviets find themselves losing they will escalate the conflict to the nuclear level. If Finite Deterrence decreases the chances of outright nuclear attacks, it increases the chance of conventional war, and conventional wars between superpowers will turn into nuclear wars.

(b)   Finite Deterrence insists on strong command and control links between the president and all strategic forces. Admittedly, communications links between simplified strategic forces are easier to maintain than links between the complex strategic forces of the Countervailing Strategy. But this concentration of authority provides a military opening for opponents. If an opponent can succeed in killing the president and secretary of defense before they delegate their authority, then commanders in the field will have neither the authority nor the physical ability to release strategic weapons. In its own way, Finite Deterrence may collapse before a decapitating first strike.

(c)   Finite Deterrence is designed to give the president time to think about what to do after the United States suffers a first strike. The president will know the condition of the country; he will know whether American cities are largely unscathed or destroyed. If they are unscathed, he will not order a second strike, for fear of provoking a third strike that will indeed destroy American cities. If they are already destroyed, he will not order a second strike because there is nothing left to save. Thus, no matter what happens, under Finite Deterrence it is irrational to launch a second strike.

If we adopt Finite Deterrence, the president will have thought these things through in advance. His potential opponents will also have thought things through, and will realize that if the American president is rational, there are no conditions in which he will launch a second strike, which means they can issue a first strike without fear of retaliation. Under Finite Deterrence, nuclear deterrence becomes incredible and fails to deter. It is no remedy to this problem to suggest that the president should become manifestly irrational. Visible irrationality in the American president will cause anxiety, and anxiety will tempt the opponent toward a preemptive first strike.

(d)   Suppose Warsaw Pact forces invade western Europe and defeat NATO forces in a conventional war. West Germany, France, the Low Countries are about to be overrun. Suppose, more fantastically, that Soviet forces using conventional weapons invade the United States and succeed in controlling the country. According to the doctrine of "no first use," even in circumstances like these the use of nuclear weapons is forbidden. But even those who agree that nuclear weapons should be a last resort might think that the imminent conquest is a time for last resorts. Otherwise, potential invaders know that they will not meet nuclear resistance, no matter what rights they violate, so long as they do not resort to nuclear weapons.

10. A CRITICISM OF FINITE DETERRENCE FROM THE LEFT
AND THREE REBUTTALS

The policy of Finite Deterrence assumes that second strike uses of nuclear weapons are morally acceptable. But even if the president directs nuclear weapons only at military forces, factories, dams, and other industrial targets, these second strikes will kill millions of people. Now, second strikes are launched after deterrence has failed, but after deterrence has failed, second strikes do very little good: the entire motive of threatening second strikes is to prevent first strikes from occurring. So a second strike will kill millions of people to no purpose, and such an act cannot be morally right.

Defenders of Finite Deterrence have developed three responses to this moral challenge.

(i.)   Some Finite Deterrence theorists argue that Finite Deterrence does not in fact *threaten* a second strike. All it demands is the *capacity* for a second strike. It is consistent with Finite Deterrence that the president not have made up his mind about what to do in the event of a first strike. It is even consistent with Finite Deterrence that the president be determined never to authorize a second strike. It achieves deterrence because an opponent could never be sure retaliation would not come, and the price of error in these circumstances is very high. Thus the policy is not committed to the actual use of nuclear weapons, though a particular president might be. Since it makes no threats, it makes no immoral threats.

(ii.)   Other Finite Deterrence theorists agree that carrying out a second strike would be morally wrong. But they insist that it is nevertheless permissible to threaten a second strike. Threatening a second strike and executing a second strike are logically distinct acts, and it is possible that the first could be morally permissible and the second morally wrong. In the case of Finite Deterrence, the threat of a second strike is permissible but the second strike itself is not. The situation is a little unusual, but not unique to nuclear confrontations: sometimes it is permissible to threaten to spank a small child when it would be morally wrong actually to spank the child. Before the second strike, then, Finite Deterrence is morally in the clear, and if it works, it will never be necessary to carry out the second strike.

(iii.)   A few Finite Deterrence theorists infer the acceptability of second strike directly from the acceptability of second-strike threats. They argue (a) that it is morally permissible to threaten a second strike since there is no other way in the nuclear age for a government to protect its citizens against first strikes; (b) that if it is morally permissible to make the threat, then it must be morally permissible to carry out the threat, since threats and acts threatened are logically connected.

For example, if I make a legitimate promise to do X under certain conditions, it is legitimate for me to carry out my promise when those conditions occur, even if carrying out the promise may have worse effects than not carrying it out. What goes for promises goes for nuclear threats. (This argument addresses both the immorality and the alleged irrationality of Finite Deterrence.)

The critics to the left of Finite Deterrence find all three rebuttals invalid.

The argument that Finite Deterrence does not involve a commitment to a second strike implies that Finite Deterrence could be just one huge bluff. But it is fantastic to suppose that the United States under Finite Deterrence could suffer a nuclear attack without replying in kind. Any president in peacetime who committed himself to not responding would be impeached. Any president in wartime who chose not to respond would be deposed. Bluffing is for the poker table. A fleet of strategic submarines, ICBMs, and strategic bombers cannot be managed on a bluff basis. Those who man the weapons will not dedicate their lives to playing games.

Thus Finite Deterrence involves an intention to launch a second strike, and this intention must be evaluated morally. Now, when we evaluate intentions morally, we cannot avoid referring to what is intended. The mere *threat* to do an act can be considered separately from the act itself, because we can make threats without intending to carry them out. But we cannot consider an *intention* separately from an act intended, since we cannot form an intention to do an act without committing ourselves to doing the act. In this case, the act is mass murder, and the intention requires a commitment to mass murder. The fact that it is unlikely that we will carry out the intention, and the fact that publicizing the intention reduces the chance that we will carry it out, are morally irrelevant. Suppose that I intend to strangle the next girl I see who is wearing a pink polka dot dress, and that I place an anonymous advertisement announcing my intention in the local newspaper. Pink polka dot dresses are rare, and my advertisement makes it even less likely that they will be worn. Nevertheless, it is immoral for me to make such a murderous commitment.

This argument infers the immorality of the intention from the immorality of the act intended. Deterrence theorists often argue the other way around, and infer the permissibility of the act intended from the permissibility of the intention. But how could it be morally permissible to intend mass murder, even if the murder is not carried out? Theorists argue that the intention to launch a second strike is justified on grounds of self-defense; but, as we have seen, self-defense justifications for any variety of nuclear deterrence are weak. Others argue that forming these second-strike intentions is justified because they reduce the risk of nuclear war. The left-wing critics of Finite Deterrence argue that it has not been shown that forming these intentions is the only way, or the best way, to reduce the risk of nuclear war. In their view, the chance of nuclear war would be less if the United States decommissioned its nuclear weapons, less than under Finite Deterrence, and much less than under the Countervailing Strategy.

Thus, most of those who criticize Finite Deterrence on moral grounds endorse the policy of Nuclear Disarmament.

11. NUCLEAR DISARMAMENT

Like Finite Deterrence theorists, supporters of Nuclear Disarmament believe that nuclear weapons are not genuine weapons. But Finite Deterrence sanctions one use of nuclear devices as legitimate: retaliation in a second strike. Nuclear disarmers argue that even *this* use of nuclear devices is immoral and dangerous, and that the simplest remedy is to decommission the devices.

Nuclear disarmers believe that such an act will *decrease* the overall risk of nuclear war. To most students of nuclear strategy, this claim is heresy. The standard view is that if the United States decommissioned its nuclear weapons, the Soviet Union would be encouraged to attack the United States, and the overall chance of nuclear war would be greatly increased. But consider the following counterarguments.

As long as the United States continues to deploy nuclear weapons, there is a chance that the United States will be the one to start a nuclear war—either by choice or by accident. Whatever that chance is, it will become zero if the United States abolishes its nuclear weapons. Consider, furthermore, that the most likely reason for a Soviet nuclear attack against the United States would be to preempt a suspected American nuclear attack against the Soviet Union. If the United States decommissioned its nuclear weapons, this reason for a Soviet nuclear attack would disappear.

The key question, then, for the policy of Nuclear Disarmament is whether these factors leading to a decreased chance of nuclear war outbalance the other factors leading to an increased chance of nuclear war. Supporters of nuclear disarmament firmly believe that they do. If you believe that the Soviet Union and the United States are equally likely to start a nuclear war, then if the American probability of starting war shrinks to zero, the Soviet probability must double if the overall chance of nuclear war is to increase. But it is hardly likely that the Soviet probability of starting nuclear war will double if the principal incentive for starting nuclear war is removed.

This argument does not show that the chance of a nuclear attack on the United States will decrease. Indeed, it is possible, given unilateral nuclear disarmament, that the chance of attack on the United States will increase. What the argument says is that with American nuclear disarmament the *overall* chance of nuclear war in the world will decrease. It is typical of supporters of nuclear disarmament that they are primarily concerned with the interests of the world as a whole, not just the interests of the United States.

Supporters of nuclear disarmament believe that on their proposal the chance of any sort of nuclear war will decrease. They also believe that the chance of a *very big* nuclear war, the sort of nuclear war that will kill at least several billion people and that might destroy the human race, will be *very much* decreased. A species-destroying nuclear war is most likely to result from a massive nuclear exchange between the superpowers, during which the United States and the Soviet Union hurl most of their nuclear arsenals at each other. This sort of massive exchange would be impossible if the United States had no nuclear weapons. It takes two sides to make a nuclear holocaust.

Nuclear disarmament by the United States would reduce the chance of the sort of nuclear war that would destroy the human species. It also would reduce the chances of the sort of nuclear war that would destroy the United States. If the United States keeps its weapons and the Soviet Union chooses to attack the United States, that attack surely will be a massive attack, designed to limit damage from an American counterstrike against the Soviet Union. If the United States had no nuclear weapons and the Soviets chose to attack the United States, it is very likely that they would use no nuclear weapons at all, or would use only a few nuclear weapons for purposes of intimidation, in order to keep radioactivity from blowing back in their direction or ruining their prize. Such demonstration bombings would cause terrible damage in the United States. But the bulk of the country would survive to resist the invader.

These arguments presume that the Soviet Union will behave in a self-serving but rational manner, even in time of war. Critics of nuclear disarmament argue that this policy might work against rational political leaders but will leave the United States helpless against an irrational opponent—a suicidal madman, for example, possessing nuclear arms and bent on sheer destruction. But the madman example backfires against its proponents. Against a nuclear madman, the Countervailing Strategy and Finite Deterrence are as helpless as Nuclear Disarmament. All they can do with a nuclear madman is blow him up *after* he has destroyed the United States. A suicidal madman does not care about dying and cannot be deterred.

Furthermore, there is always the possibility that the madman might be American. During the tension-filled days of the Watergate scandal, Richard Nixon terrified congressional visitors by remarking, "I can go into that room, pick up a phone, and 20 minutes later 50 million people will be dead" (Phil Sanford, "Who Pushes the Button?" *Parade*, 28 March 1976). Shortly thereafter, White House staff ordered the Pentagon not to act on any "unusual messages" coming from the White House without checking first with Alexander Haig. American nuclear deterrence cannot control a mad American leader. Only nuclear disarmament can, by depriving the madman of nuclear arms.

Obviously, the principal moral argument for nuclear disarmament is that it serves the interests of the human race by diminishing the risk of nuclear war, and by substantially diminishing the risk of apocalyptic nuclear war. But nuclear disarmers feel that nuclear deterrence is also essentially *unfair*, in that nuclear deterrence requires a nation to maintain a nuclear weapons policy that it does not wish other nations to emulate. If the Countervailing Strategy is morally permissible, then the United States should wish that all nations develop nuclear arms and maintain a Countervailing Strategy of their own. If Finite Deterrence is morally permissible, the United States should wish all nations to develop nuclear weapons and maintain Finite Deterrence. But few Americans would be happy in a world of 125 or so nuclear powers. Apparently, the United States wishes other nations to practice nuclear abstinence when it is not prepared to accept abstinence itself. Such behavior is unjust.

Finally, many nuclear disarmers believe that American nuclear weapons violate the rights of people in nonnuclear nations by imposing risks on them that they are unable to reciprocate. If American nuclear weapons are used in quantity, they will, directly or indirectly, kill millions of people in nonaligned nations, poison their soil, and disrupt their genetic heritage. The damage of nuclear war is so great that it is a violation of rights to impose the risk of such damage. But if it is a violation of rights to impose these risks, then it is morally wrong to impose them, even if one imposes them in a good cause, and even if imposing them benefits the world as a whole. Nuclear disarmers do not agree with Finite Deterrence or with the Countervailing Strategy that nuclear weapons serve a good end. But even if they did, the alleged good end could not justify such immoral means.

12. CRITICISMS OF NUCLEAR DISARMAMENT

(a) The French philosopher Jean-Jacques Rousseau remarked about a scheme for world government that its only flaw was that no prince in the world would ever accept it. Much the same can be said about unilateral nuclear disarmament: none of the nuclear powers will disarm if the others do not. In particular, the United States surely will not give up its nuclear weapons if the Soviet Union retains nuclear weapons. This is not just the attitude of American leaders. It is the attitude of the vast majority of the American people. Even if the arguments of unilateral disarmers are valid, their proposal is impossibly utopian.

(b) If the United States gives up nuclear weapons and the Soviet Union does not, then the Soviet Union can blackmail the United States into any concession it desires, simply by threatening to destroy American cities. It would hardly be necessary for the Soviet Union to carry out these threats: in the absence of any American ability to retaliate, the credibility of Soviet threats would be apparent and the blackmail would invariably succeed.

(c)   If the United States gives up its weapons unilaterally, then the allies of the United States would consider their security to be in jeopardy. They would move to take up the nuclear slack, beefing up their own nuclear arsenals or acquiring nuclear weapons for the first time. In particular, if the United States had no nuclear weapons in place against the Soviet Union, many people in West Germany would demand German nuclear armament, and German nuclear armament would probably raise the risk of nuclear war more than American nuclear disarmament could reduce it.

(d)   If unilateral disarmers find nuclear weapons so threatening to the welfare of the human race, their goal should be the abolition of all nuclear weapons, not just American nuclear weapons. But unilateral decommissioning of American nuclear weapons makes world nuclear disarmament less likely, since the strongest incentive that one could give to the Soviet Union to give up its nuclear weapons would be the realization that the Americans will give up nuclear weapons *if and only if* they give up theirs.

(e)   Nuclear disarmers make much of the risks that American nuclear weapons inflict on nonaligned nations. They declare that inflicting these risks is unfair. But it is equally unfair that the Soviets should keep their nuclear weapons if the Americans give theirs up. In that case, the Soviets would be inflicting on the United States the same unreciprocated risks that the United States—and all the other nuclear powers—inflict on nonnuclear states. To adopt nuclear disarmament, then, would be to make the United States a victim of injustice.

(f)   Some nuclear disarmers concede that nuclear disarmament would be a good thing for the world but a bad thing for the United States. But the American president and other elected American leaders are bound—morally bound—by their role as political leaders to look out for the interests of the United States. The president, as president, cannot place the interests of non-Americans above the interests of Americans. But this is what nuclear disarmament asks him to do if, as many believe, nuclear disarmament would be a relatively bad thing for the United States but a good thing for the world in general.

13.   ARMS CONTROL AND MULTILATERAL DISARMAMENT

Most Americans believe that the United States should not give up its nuclear weapons if the Soviets keep theirs. But the majority of Americans believe that the United States should give up some nuclear weapons if the Soviets also give up some. At the Reykjavik summit meeting in 1986, leaders of both superpowers toyed with the idea of a step-by-step elimination of

American and Soviet ballistic missiles. Many Americans supported this initiative, and many Americans think that it would be a good idea for the United States to give up all its nuclear weapons if the other nuclear powers gave up all of theirs.

The attraction of such bilateral and multilateral reductions is obvious. Each superpower has had the experience of investing heavily in a weapons system that was supposed to provide increased security, only to find its security decreased when the other side constructed the same system. In such cases, it would have been far better for both sides to agree not to build the systems in the first place. MIRV provides perhaps the best example of a system built and then regretted; the ABM treaty provides the best example of an agreement not to build.

The two superpowers have a common interest in agreements not to build parallel strategic systems. Yet in 30 years of arms control negotiations the two superpowers have succeeded only in constructing a hot line, banning nuclear tests in the atmosphere, limiting ABM systems, eliminating strategically superfluous medium range missiles, and setting modest and temporary limits on totals of strategic missiles. Each side has a military-industrial complex with a vested interest in military spending, regardless of long-term negative effects. Each side distrusts the other, and fears that the other side will use the agreement to gain some special advantage. But perhaps the greatest obstacle to mutual agreements is that each side shares the assumption of the Countervailing Strategy that a nuclear weapons system can provide a military advantage—at least until your opponent builds one of his own.

If nuclear weapons systems convey military advantages, then each side has an irresistible argument for building weapons systems. Call a weapons system W. Either my opponent will build W or he won't. If he doesn't and I do, I will have an advantage. If he does and I don't, I will be at a disadvantage. Thus, I should build W no matter what my opponent does. The argument works for both sides, so both build W, even though both realize they would be better off if they chose not to build. (Game theorists call such situations "prisoner's dilemmas.")

The prisoner's dilemma argument fails, however, on the assumptions of Finite Deterrence. Provided we retain the ability to launch a second strike, we gain no advantage by adding on nuclear weapons systems, nor do we stand at a disadvantage if the Soviets build nuclear weapons systems we do not have. If we have superfluous nuclear weapons systems, we have an incentive to negotiate their removal in return for similar reductions on the other side. If we do not succeed, we should scrap them anyway. For the countervailing strategy, arms control is a sacrifice at best and a swindle at worst. For Finite Deterrence, it is a liquidation sale.

Finite Deterrence and mutual nuclear disarmament go hand in hand—up to a point. That stopping point is the point at which each side has reduced its nuclear arsenal to the small set of nuclear weapons prescribed by Finite Deterrence. Beyond that point, each superpower fears that if it gives up its nuclear weapons, the other side might gain a tremendous advantage by hiding a few nuclear missiles in caves. Furthermore, even if two nuclear powers wanted to give up their nuclear weapons, each side might fear that the other has the ability to *rebuild* nuclear weapons faster than it can rebuild them. Can two nuclear powers with small arsenals find a way to make a final and permanent reduction to zero nuclear weapons on each side?

Each side fears that the other may conceal its last few nuclear weapons. One way to allay this fear would be for some third power—a world government, perhaps—to assure the United States and the Soviet Union that if either makes a military move using nuclear weapons, *it* will take reprisals against the offender. The United States and the Soviet Union might even agree to turn their nuclear weapons over to this third power. But supporters of nuclear disarmament are unlikely to be happy with this idea. Not only are world governments dreams for the distant future, but the idea of a world government that goes around making nuclear threats looks to nuclear disarmers like a continuation of the present reign of nuclear terror.

Nuclear disarmers will propose only remedies that do not themselves require nuclear weapons. Rather than a world government armed with nuclear bombs, nuclear disarmers would prefer the creation of an international authority with the power to control the fissionable material from which nuclear weapons are made. Such a proposal was developed by the United States in 1946 and placed before the United Nations, where it was rejected by the Soviet Union, that is, by Stalin. But Stalin is long dead, and the Soviets, chastened by their experiences with the Chernobyl disaster, seem increasingly to share the view that nuclear weapons provide more insecurity than security. They proposed and unilaterally maintained a moratorium on nuclear weapons testing from 1985 to 1987, and have even gone so far as to invite on-site inspection of Soviet nuclear weapons tests by Western scientific observers. In this new context, nuclear disarmers argue that the time is ripe for the United States to press once again for the international supervision of the materials needed to produce nuclear weapons.

14.   LAST WORDS FROM THE COUNTERVAILING STRATEGY

The Countervailing Strategy is portrayed by its opponents as an expensive and fruitless attempt to gain superiority in the nuclear arms race. Its opponents propose a shift from nuclear arms toward conventional methods of defense. But nuclear weapons and nuclear weapons delivery systems take up only 10 percent of the U. S. defense budget. The other 90 percent goes for conventional arms. Any shift from nuclear arms to conventional arms will cause the defense budget to go up, not down. Furthermore, the changes under way in strategic weapons under the Countervailing Strategy are not attempts at superiority but prudent modernizations of aging forces, which contain bombers from the 1950s, and missiles and submarines from the 1960s.

It is often alleged that the goal of the Countervailing Strategy is a nuclear first strike against the Soviet Union. But there is nothing in the Countervailing Strategy that makes a first strike possible. Even the most ardent anti-Communists recognize that a full launch of all nuclear weapons against the Soviet Union cannot remove the small but substantial chance that a single Soviet warhead would survive and strike the United States. That single warhead could kill 20 times more Americans than died in all the wars the United States ever fought. No American president has shown any interest in taking this risk; all presidents thus far have rejected all suggestions along these lines and have concentrated instead on measures to prevent accidental or unauthorized launches of nuclear weapons. The nuclear stalemate between the superpowers is very stable, and all present and planned changes in nuclear weapons do not move either side closer to the reality of a first strike against the other. But should war begin, the United States needs the full range of nuclear weapons to fight, fight as cleanly as nuclear weapons permit, and win.

15.   LAST WORDS FROM STRATEGIC DEFENSE

The critics of Strategic Defense say that strategic defenses can never be built well enough to stop a first strike. In a sense this is true, since no system can be constructed that will surely stop every incoming enemy weapon. But in another sense this is false, because strategic defenses *can* be constructed that will be good enough to stop an enemy from *considering* a first strike. A nuclear opponent facing American strategic defenses cannot be certain what its nuclear weapons will achieve; in particular, it cannot know whether anything it might hope to achieve by a first strike will be successful, given American strategic defenses. Pondering the risks, it will give up the first-strike plans. Likewise, Soviet defensive systems would cause the United States to give up its first-strike plans, if it had any. The difficulties that strategic defenses pose for successful nuclear offense are greater than the difficulties involved in creating these defenses. Thus, strategic defenses are not destabilizing; the uncertainties they cause create a deeper level of stability.

16. LAST WORDS FROM FINITE DETERRENCE

Many critics of Finite Deterrence claim that this system involves a unique commitment to mass murder. But Finite Deterrence cannot involve more of a commitment to mass murder than the Countervailing Strategy, since the use of nuclear weapons according to Finite Deterrence will kill no more people than the use of nuclear weapons according to the Countervailing Strategy. Both strategies call for the use of nuclear weapons against military targets, but supporters of both strategies know that use of nuclear weapons against such targets may kill millions of innocent bystanders.

The potential death of millions of bystanders leads supporters of Nuclear Disarmament to condemn both the Countervailing Strategy and Finite Deterrence. But under Finite Deterrence, nuclear weapons are to be used only as a last resort, and in fact it is extremely unlikely that they will ever be used. Murder is the deliberate or reckless killing of the innocent. Finite Deterrence does not deliberately aim at the innocent, nor can actions that have a low probability of killing anyone, and are designed solely to prevent nuclear war, be described as reckless.

Furthermore, if Finite Deterrence or any other policy is to be described as "murderous," it must be morally responsible for any deaths it might cause. But, under Finite Deterrence, if any Russians are killed by American nuclear weapons, they will be killed only after a Soviet nuclear attack on the United States. The Soviets will have attacked first, knowing full well that the United States will retaliate against this attack. If any bystanders are killed, the Soviets, not the Americans, are responsible for these deaths.

The Soviets will be responsible for deaths caused by American bombs, even though the Americans could have chosen not to drop them. We have here a chain of causes, beginning with a Soviet attack followed by American retaliation, followed by Russian deaths. The Soviets had no right to attack the United States, but the Americans had a right to take such steps as would reduce the chance of Soviet nuclear attack. These steps necessarily involved setting in place the machinery of retaliation. Thus, in the chain of causation, the morally legitimate American act is not responsible for the tragic result; the illegitimate Soviet act is. If any murder has occurred, the murderer is the one who launched the first strike.

Finite Deterrence requires a few, simple, invulnerable nuclear weapons, the very presence of which deters a nuclear attack. Critics of Finite Deterrence point out that it would be irrational to use these weapons after a first strike, but the truth of this does not undercut the effectiveness of Finite Deterrence. Even if retaliation is irrational, no enemy can be sure that the United States will perform only rational acts, particularly after the unique trauma of suffering nuclear attack. The price of being wrong about what the United States might do after a nuclear attack, large or small, is so great that the chance of a Soviet first strike under Finite Deterrence is vanishingly small.

17. LAST WORDS ABOUT NUCLEAR DISARMAMENT

Supporters of nuclear disarmament are often portrayed as irresponsible fanatics who care only for the sacred cause of nuclear disarmament and pay no attention to other values, such as political freedom. They are accused of feeling that somehow the world would be better off if the United States were weak and the Soviet Union were strong. Their proposals—it is alleged—would allow the Soviet Union to blackmail the United States at will.

Supporters of nuclear disarmament protest that these arguments confuse nuclear disarmament with pacifism. Nuclear disarmament does not imply general and complete disarmament. Nuclear disarmers believe that nuclear devices are not weapons and that reliance on nuclear devices is a sign of national weakness, not military strength. Nuclear devices cannot be integrated into usable, effective fighting plans. And if they are reserved for purposes of retaliation only, when the time comes to use them, it will be too late.

Most nuclear disarmers believe in a strong defense. But they believe that the only strong defense is a nonnuclear defense. They want the Army, Navy, Air Force, and Marines to be trained in the use of weapons that will win military objectives, not blow up everything in sight. Many nuclear disarmers also believe that the civilian populations of nation-states, especially the states of western Europe, should be trained in the techniques of political resistance, which could create such difficulties for occupying forces as to make the conquest of these nations manifestly not worth the trouble. Sweden, Switzerland, and Yugoslavia have already taken serious steps in this direction. Nuclear disarmers, then, are not demanding sacrifices in American strength, or forcing the president to violate his oath.

Opponents of nuclear disarmament claim that nonnuclear forces, however strong, cannot withstand nuclear attack and cannot repel nuclear blackmail. But nuclear weapons provide no magic remedy against nuclear blackmail. A blackmailer with nuclear weapons can effectively threaten any nuclear power by making it appear that he does not care about dying. Blackmail is essentially a contest of wills, and the problem is solved by willpower, not by missiles and nuclear bombs.

A nonnuclear nation with confidence in the fighting effectiveness of its armed forces is unlikely to collapse before nuclear blackmail. From 1945 to 1949 the United States had nuclear weapons and the Soviet Union had none. This did not stop the Soviet Union from blocking elections in Poland, subverting Czechoslovakia, and consolidating control of eastern Europe. In those years Stalin knew that any use of nuclear weapons against Russia could be countered by moving the Red Army into Western Europe. There is no reason why a nonnuclear United States, confronted by a nuclear opponent, could not exhibit similar strength of will in the service of democratic causes.

If the United States "transarmed," substituting effective conventional weaponry for its present blind reliance on nuclear devices, other states would have scant motive to develop or increase nuclear forces. The British French, and Chinese have in deed, if not in word, endorsed Finite Deterrence: they retain small arsenals as a last-resort deterrent against Soviet attack. They will retain exactly the same deterrent—no more, no less—regardless of whether the United States arms or disarms.

Likewise, whether West Germany acquires nuclear weapons does not depend on American strategic decisions: it depends on internal politics in West Germany and on the perceived threat of Soviet invasion. Since the Berlin Wall was built in 1961, this threat of invasion has been considered minimal, and the volume of trade between West Germany and the Soviet bloc is now so great that the real chance of Soviet invasion is less than ever. Unlike their critics, nuclear disarmers are not so blind as to think that everything that happens in the world depends on what the United States does first.

In a world in which some sovereign states possess nuclear weapons and in which even "conventional" wars can claim millions of lives, it is crucial to prevent all wars, not just nuclear wars. The new conventional forces that nuclear disarmament will substitute for nuclear weapons must provide a secure defense, without increasing the insecurity of nearby countries. They must provide defense without offense, security without threats. The design of such forces is a delicate matter. Fixed emplacements provide defense without offense, but trust in fixed emplacements died with the Maginot Line. On the other hand, too much emphasis on penetration toward the invader's homeland—along the lines of NATO's current "deep strike" strategy—sends the wrong signal to the opponent and tempts military leaders toward maneuvers as catastrophic as MacArthur's plunge toward the Yalu River in Korea. What must be stressed are mobile antitank weapons and other antiarmor devices that cancel high technology with low cost, and the development of tactics using dispersed but highly mobile forces.

Such forces may appear light relative to invading heavy armor, but to be safe from conquest, a country need not shatter the invading army or destroy the invader's country; it need prove only that the cost of conquest far outweighs any expectable gains. Low-tech nonnuclear forces are best suited to the task of defense without offense. Nuclear weapons are eminently unsuitable, since nuclear weapons in any configuration will always be perceived as a threat.

Since nuclear disarmers want military forces used only to forestall conquest, they reject the view that American forces should be used to intervene around the world in defense of American interests. If such interventions do moral good, then this is a moral good that nuclear disarmament must forgo. But in the court of world opinion, American interventions in the nuclear era—in Iran, in Guatemala, in Vietnam, in Chile, for example—have in general been viewed as moral evils. If nuclear disarmament produces a new isolationism, and prevents us from doing good, it also prevents us from doing harm.

Defense without offense does not require that the United States give up all influence—only influence based on the threat of force. Obviously one can influence people not only by threatening them with some harm but also by promising them some good. In the future, if there is one, it is not clear that the most influential countries will remain the ones that can threaten world destruction. In the 1940s, the Japanese tried to control East Asia by building bigger battleships. Fortunately and predictably, they failed. Forty years later they have gained worldwide influence by building better cameras. The moral gap between the two methods is plain to the Japanese, but the ethical message does not seem to have penetrated the nuclear powers, East or West.

Nuclear disarmament is derided as utopian. But it was utopian in the early nineteenth century to call for abolition of slavery. Yet slavery was abolished, and it is difficult to imagine now how it was tolerated at all. Nuclear disarmers feel that nuclear weapons are as wicked as slavery, and they argue that if slavery could be abolished, so can nuclear weapons. They pray that abolition will not require a global Civil War.

18. SUGGESTIONS FOR FURTHER READING

The Elements of Nuclear Strategy

For a description of the effects of the Hiroshima bombing, see references to Ch. 4, Sec. "American Bombing and Hiroshima."

Extensive information about nuclear weapons and delivery systems is presented in *Nuclear Weapons Databooks*, ed. T. Cochran et al. (Cambridge, MA: 1984–). For an up-to-date listing of the world's nuclear forces, see *The Military Balance*, published each year by the Institute of Strategic Studies (London).

The figure of 60,000 nuclear warheads is taken from a U. S. Department of Defense Study. See Richard Halloran, "Soviets Said to Lead by 8,000 Warheads," *New York Times*, (18 June 1984).

The Countervailing Strategy Defended

For descriptions of the Countervailing Strategy, see Desmond Ball, *Targeting for Strategic Deterrence* (London: Institute for Strategic Studies, 1983); Jeffrey Richelson, "PD-59, NSDD-13, and the Reagan Strategic Modernization Program," *Journal of Strategic Studies* 6, no. 2 (June 1983); and Michio Kaku and Daniel Axelrod, *To Win a Nuclear War* (Boston: South End Press, 1986).

An articulate defense of the countervailing strategy is provided by Secretary of Defense Harold Brown in *Annual Report of the Secretary of Defense to the Congress of the United States for The Fiscal Year 1979–80*; (Washington, D.C.: U.S. Government Printing Office, 1979); and by Colin Gray and Keith Payne, "Victory Is Possible," *Foreign Policy* (Summer 1980). The argument that the countervailing strategy and its ancestors have "worked" to keep the peace is given by Caspar Weinberger in "Remarks by the Secretary of Defense to the Massachusetts Medical Society," *New England Journal of Medicine* 307, no. 12 (16 September 1982); and in Joseph Nye, Jr., *Nuclear Ethics* (New York: Free Press, 1986).

Criticisms of the Countervailing Strategy from the Right

For the argument that current nuclear policy leaves the United States "defenseless," see Donald Graham, *Shall America Be Defended?* (New York: Arlington House, 1979) and *We Must Defend America* (Chicago: Regnery Gateway, 1983). For failure of escalation dominance under current policy, see Colin Gray, *Nuclear Strategy and Strategic Planning* (Philadelphia: Foreign Policy Research Institute, 1984). For remarks about seizing the initiative in nuclear war, see the quotations from Curtis LeMay in David Alan Rosenberg, "A Smoking Radiating Ruin in About Two Hours: American Plans for Nuclear War with the Soviet Union 1954–55," *International Security* 6. no. 3 (Winter 1981–1982). For the argument that the Countervailing Strategy puts America at risk for the defense of Germany, see the essay by Eric Mack in *Defending a Free Society*, ed. Robert W. Poole, Jr. (Lexington, MA: Lexington Books, 1984).

The Case for Strategic Defense

The classic argument for Strategic Defense is Donald Brennan, "The Case for Missile Defense," *Foreign Affairs* (April 1969). For justifications of current proposals for strategic defense, see Donald Graham, *The Nonnuclear Defense of Cities* (Cambridge, MA: Abt Books, 1983); Ronald Reagan, "Speech on Military Spending and a New Defense" [the "Star Wars" speech], *New York Times* (24 March 1983); George Keyworth, "The Case for Strategic Defense: An Option for a Disarmed World," *Issues in Science and Technology* (Fall 1984); *The President's Strategic Defense Initiative* (Washington, DC: The White House, January 1985); and Alan Chalfont *Star Wars: Suicide or Survival?* (Boston: Little, Brown, 1986).

The argument that Strategic Defense is morally superior on grounds of the right to self-defense is found in Jerry Pournelle and Dean Ing, *Mutual Assured Survival* (New York: Baen Books, 1984); and in Robert Jastrow, *How to Make Nuclear Weapons Obsolete* (Boston: Little, Brown, 1985). The moral arguments for strategic defense are analyzed from all sides in *Ethics and Strategic Defense*, ed. Douglas Lackey (Belmont, CA: Wadsworth, 1988).

The Case Against Strategic Defense

The technical and strategic arguments against strategic defense are assembled in Union of Concerned Scientists, *The Fallacy of Star Wars* (New York: Vintage, 1984); Ashton Carter, *Ballistic Missile Defense Technologies* (Washington, DC: U.S. Congress, Office of Technology Assessment, 1984); and in Robert M. Bowman, *Star Wars: A Defense Expert's Case Against the Strategic Defense Initiative* (Los Angeles: Tarcher, 1986). The argument that strategic defense is a move toward a first-strike system is given in E. P. Thompson et al., *Star Wars* (New York: Pantheon Books, 1985); and in Michio Kaku and Daniel Axelrod, *To Win a Nuclear War*. A game-theoretic argument that Strategic Defense will produce more offense, not more defense,' is given by Gregory Kavka, "Space War Ethics," *Ethics* (April 1985). The moral case for Strategic Defense is rebutted by Kavka in "A Critique of Pure Defense," *Journal of Philosophy* (November 1986); and in the articles by Douglas Lackey, Steven Lee, and Henry Shue in *The Philosophical Forum* (Autumn 1986).

Criticisms of the Countervailing Strategy from the Left

The arguments for the essentially conservative character of Soviet foreign policy are given in George P. Kennan, *The Nuclear Delusion* (New York: Viking, 1982). The argument that the use of tactical and theater nuclear weapons is essentially suicidal is given in Solly Zuckerman, *Nuclear Illusion and Reality* (New York: Viking, 1982). Arguments that nuclear war cannot be controlled are in Desmond Ball, *Can Nuclear War Be Controlled?* (London: Institute for Strategic Studies, 1979); and Ian Clark, *Limited Nuclear War: Political Theory and War Conventions* (Princeton, NJ: Princeton University Press, 1982). The pressure under the Countervailing Strategy toward preemptive use of nuclear weapons is described in Robert Aldridge, *First Strike! The Pentagon's Strategy for Nuclear War* (London: Pluto Press, 1983).

The arms race aspects of the Countervailing Strategy are described in Louis Rene Beres, *Mimicking Sisyphus: America's Countervailing Nuclear Strategy* (Lexington, MA: Lexington Books, 1982). The problem of accidental nuclear war is surveyed in Daniel Frei, *Risks of Unintentional Nuclear War* (Totowa, NJ: Allanheld, Osmun, 1983); Dan Ford, *The Button* (New York: Simon and Schuster, 1985); and in *Peace Research Review* 10, no.3 and 10, no. 4 (1986).

A comprehensive rebuttal of the strategic arguments for the Countervailing Strategy is Robert Jervis, *The Illogic of Nuclear Strategy* (Ithaca, NY: Cornell University Press, 1983).

Two Views About Atomic Bombs

A detailed review of the development of nuclear-war fighting theory is David Alan Rosenberg, "The Origins of Overkill: Nuclear Weapons and American Strategy," *International Security* 7, no. 4 (Spring 1983). See also Kaku and Axelrod, *To Win a Nuclear War.*

The view that nuclear weapons are not genuine weapons is defended in Kennan, *The Nuclear Delusion*; Robert S. McNamara, "The Military Role of Nuclear Weapons," *Foreign Affairs* 62, no. 1 (Fall 1983); and Morton Halperin, *Nuclear Fallacy* (Cambridge, MA: Ballinger, 1987).

The quotation about Nagasaki is from W. H. Lawrence, "Dead Nagasaki Seen From a B-17," *New York Times* (27 August 1945).

Arguments about the special character of the effects of nuclear weapons are in Jonathan Schell, *The Fate of the Earth* (New York: Knopf, 1982); and in the articles by Jefferson McMahan and others in *Nuclear Weapons and the Future of Humanity*, ed. Avner Cohen and Steven Lee (Totowa, NJ: Rowman and Allanheld, 1986).

The argument that smoke and dust from nuclear explosions could generate a "nuclear winter" is given by R. P. Turco, O. B. Toon, T. P. Ackerman, J. B. Pollack, and Carl Sagan in articles in *Science* 222, no. 4630 (December 1983) and *Scientific American* (August 1984). See also P. Ehrlich et al., *The Cold and the Dark* (New York: W. W. Norton, 1984). For critical assessment see Stanley L. Thompson and Stephen H. Schneider, "Nuclear Winter Reappraised," *Foreign Affairs* 64, no. 5 (Summer 1986).

Finite Deterrence

The weapons systems required for Finite Deterrence are described in Richard Garwin, "Reducing Dependence on Nuclear Weapons: A Second Nuclear Regime," in *Nuclear Weapons and World Politics*, ed. David Gompert et al. (New York: McGraw-Hill, 1977); Boston Study Group, *Winding Down: The Price of Defense* (San Francisco: W. H. Freeman, 1978); Harold Feiveson, Richard Ullman, and Frank Van Hippel, "Reducing U. S. and Soviet Nuclear Arsenals," *Bulletin of the Atomic Scientists* 41, no. 7 (August 1985): 144–151; Richard Ullman, "Nuclear Arms: How Big a Cut?" *New York Times Magazine* (17 November 1986); and Halperin, *Nuclear Fallacy.*

The possibility of defending western Europe with nonnuclear weapons is optimistically discussed in John J. Mearsheimer, *Conventional Deterrence* (Ithaca, NY: Cornell University Press, 1983); and Alternative Defence Commission, *Defense Without the Bomb* (London: Taylor and Francis, 1983). For a discussion of related issues, see McGeorge Bundy, George Kennan, Robert McNamara, and Gerard Smith, "Nuclear Weapons and the Atlantic

Alliance," *Foreign Affairs* (Spring 1982); *The European Security Study: Strengthening Conventional Deterrence in Europe: Proposals for the 1980's* (New York: St. Martin's Press, 1983); and *NATO and the 'No First Use' Question*, ed. Leon V. Sigal (Washington, DC: Brookings Institution, 1984).

Perhaps the best array of secular moral arguments for a system like Finite Deterrence is Gregory Kavka, "Nuclear Deterrence: Some Moral Perplexities," in *The Security Gamble*, ed. Douglas Maclean (Totowa, NJ: Rowman and Allanheld, 1984). Arguments for something like Finite Deterrence on more religious grounds were endorsed by the National Council of Catholic Bishops in the celebrated pastoral letter "The Challenge of Peace," *Origins* (3 May 1983).

Criticisms of Finite Deterrence from the Right

The argument that Finite Deterrence increases the risks of conventional wars, which then escalate to the nuclear level, is given in Colin Gray, *The MX ICBM and National Security* (New York: Praeger, 1981).

The problem of a "decapitating" strike against American strategic forces is discussed in John Steinbruner "Nuclear Decapitation," *Foreign Policy* 45 (Winter 1981–1982); and Bruce Blair, *Strategic Command and Control* (Washington, DC: Brookings Institution, 1985).

The argument that nuclear weapons provide every nuclear nation with a guarantee against conquest was developed in the 1960s in Pierre Gallois, *The Balance of Terror* (Boston: Houghton Mifflin, 1961); Karl Kaiser et al., "Nuclear Weapons and the Preservation of Peace: A German Response to 'No First Use,'" *Foreign Affairs* (Summer 1982); and NATO commander Bernard Rogers, "The NATO Alliance: Prescriptions for a Difficult Decade," *Foreign Affairs* (Summer 1982).

Criticisms of Finite Deterrence from the Left

Arguments that Finite Deterrence fails to address the essentially murderous character of nuclear weapons are assembled in Richard Falk and Robert Lifton, *Indefensible Weapons* (New York: Harper and Row, 1983). The argument that even Finite Deterrence involves morally impermissible threats is presented in David Hoekema, "The Moral Status of Nuclear Deterrent Threats," *Social Philosophy and Policy* (Autumn 1985). But see Anthony Kenny, *The Logic of Deterrence* (Chicago: University of Chicago Press, 1985); and James Sterba, "How to Achieve Nuclear Deterrence Without Threatening Nuclear Destruction," in *The Ethics of War and Nuclear Deterrence*, ed. James Sterba (Belmont CA: Wadsworth, 1985), for the argument that Finite Deterrence need not involve murderous intentions.

The idea that Finite Deterrence functions "existentially" via capacities, not intentions, is given in McGeorge Bundy, "Existential Deterrence and Its Consequences," in *The Security Gamble*, ed. Maclean. The thesis that "intending X" and "doing X" are morally independent is defended in Gregory Kavka, "Some Paradoxes of Deterrence," *Journal of Philosophy* (June 1978). The idea that if intending X is morally good, then doing X must be morally good is outlined in David Gauthier, "Deterrence, Maximization, and Rationality," *Ethics* (April 1984).

Nuclear Disarmament

The argument that the policy of second-strike deterrence increases the risk of nuclear war is developed for the British deterrent in Jefferson McMahan, *British Nuclear Weapons: For and Against* (London: Junction Books, 1981); and for nuclear deterrents in general in Douglas Lackey, *Moral Principles and Nuclear Weapons* (Totowa, NJ: Rowman and Allanheld, 1984). The argument that nuclear disarmament is necessary to forestall apocalyptic nuclear war is developed in Lackey's "Missiles and Morals," *Philosophy and Public Affairs* (Summer 1982). The argument that nuclear deterrence, when restricted to the superpowers, is unfair to smaller countries is presented in Lackey's *Moral Principles and Nuclear Weapons*. The argument that it violates the rights of innocent parties to be free from nuclear risks is developed in Lackey's "Immoral Risks," *Social Philosophy and Policy* (Autumn 1985) and "Taking Risks Seriously," *Journal of Philosophy* (November 1986).

Arguments for nuclear disarmament on the basis of Christian ethics are presented by the United Methodist Council of Bishops in a pastoral letter and foundation document entitled *In Defense of Creation* (Nashville, TN: Graded Press, 1986). Other Christian arguments for nuclear disarmament are collected in *The Moral Rejection of Nuclear Deterrence*, ed. James E. Will (New York: Friendship Press, 1985).

Criticism of Nuclear Disarmament

Criticisms of nuclear disarmament from a liberal perspective are in Leon Wieseltier, *Nuclear War, Nuclear Peace* (New York: Holt, Rinehart, and Winston, 1983); and Joseph Nye, Jr., *Nuclear Ethics*. Conservative criticisms are in Michael Novak, *Moral Clarity in the Nuclear Age* (Nashville, TN: Nelson, 1983); and James Child, *Nuclear War: The Moral Dimension* (New Brunswick, NJ: Transaction Books, 1986). Many of the criticisms directed against the National Council of Catholic Bishops' stand on nuclear war in *The Catholic Bishops and Nuclear War*, ed. Judith Dwyer (Washington, DC: Georgetown University Press, 1984), apply also to nuclear disarmament. The argument that the president has a special moral duty to prefer American lives to non-American lives is given by Michael Bayles in *Nuclear War: Philosophical Perspectives*, ed. Michael Fox and Leo Groarke (New York: Peter Lang, 1985). For further criticism of unilateral disarmament, see Gregory Kavka, "Doubts About Unilateral Disarmament," and Russell

Hardin, "Unilateral vs. Multi-lateral Disarmament," both in *Philosophy and Public Affairs* (Summer 1983).

Arms Control and Multilateral Disarmament

For an account of the maneuvering that led to the SALT I agreements, see John Newhouse, *Cold Dawn: The Story of SALT* (New York: Holt Rinehart, and Winston, 1973). For a skeptical view of the superpowers' commitment to bilateral disarmament, see Alva Myrdal, *The Game of Disarmament: How the U. S. and the U.S.S.R. Run the Arms Race* (New York: Pantheon, 1977).

On the assumptions of the Countervailing Strategy, the superpowers are in a prisoner's dilemma regarding strategic arms. Ways out of the prisoner's dilemma that do not require coercion by third parties are described in Michael Taylor, *Anarchy and Cooperation* (New York: Wiley, 1976); Robert Axelrod, *The Evolution of Cooperation* (New York: Basic Books, 1984); and Steven Brams, *Superpower Games* (New Haven: Yale University Press, 1985).

The tragic history of the Baruch Plan for the internationalization of atomic weapons is described in Gregg Herken, *The Winning Weapon* (New York: Knopf, 1980); and in Larry G. Gerber, "The Baruch Plan and the Cold War," *Diplomatic History* 6 (Winter 1982).

Last Words from the Countervailing Strategy

The argument that high-accuracy weapons do not present first-strike threats when deployed in small numbers was used by the blue-ribbon Scowcroft Commission as an argument for building the MX. See transcript excerpts *New York Times* (12 April 1983).

Last Words from Strategic Defense

The argument that strategic defenses stabilize superpower relations by generating uncertainty seems to have originated with Herman Kahn in "The Case for a Thin System," in *Why ABM?* ed. J. Holst and W. Schneider (New York: Pergamon Press, 1969).

Last Words from Finite Deterrence

A version of this argument about the right to inflict self-protective risks (with a warning *not* to apply it to nuclear deterrence!) is developed in Warren Quinn, "The Right to Threaten and the Right to Punish," *Philosophy and Public Affairs* (Fall 1985).

Last Words About Nuclear Disarmament

The difficulties of succeeding at nuclear blackmail are described by Thomas Schelling vis-à-vis terrorists in "Thinking About Nuclear Terrorism," *International Security* (Spring 1982); and by Jefferson McMahan vis-à-vis nation-states in "Nuclear Blackmail," in *Dangers of Deterrence*, ed. Kay Pole and Nigel Blake (London: Routledge and Kegan Paul, 1983).

For accounts of "defense without offense," see *Defence Without the Bomb*; and Dietrich Fischer, *Preventing War in the Nuclear Age* (Totowa, NJ: Rowman and Allanheld, 1984). For the tactics of civilian resistance, see Anders Boserup and Andrew Mack, *War Without Weapons: Non-Violence in National Defense* (New York: Schocken Books, 1984); and Gene Sharp, *Making Europe Unconquerable: The Potential of Civilian Based Deterrence and Defense* (London: Taylor and Francis, 1985).

INDEX